The Golem Bride:
A Tale of Eliyahu Baal Shem

by

BARAK A. BASSMAN

TELEMACHUS PRESS

THE GOLEM BRIDE:
A TALE OF ELIYAHU BAAL SHEM

Cover designed by Telemachus Press, LLC

Cover art:
Copyright ©iStock/478339762/uncan1890
Copyright ©iStock/1132242176/suteishi

Publishing services by Telemachus Press, LLC
7652 Sawmill Road
Suite 304
Dublin, Ohio 43016
http://www.telemachuspress.com

ISBN: 978-1-965121-31-3 (eBook)
ISBN: 978-1-965121-32-0 (Paperback)

Library of Congress Control Number: 2025915257

Version 2025.07.17

Table of Contents

The Golem Bride:
A Tale of Eliyahu Baal Shem

I. A Loney Old Mystic

RABBI ELIYAHU BAAL Shem was sighing gently, alone on a bench on his dilapidated porch in the *shtetl* of C. Although his house had once been so noisy that it drove him to distraction, his wife Esther, who used to make such a racket in the kitchen, had long ago passed on to the next world, and his four brilliant sons had scattered to the winds, settling into rabbinates of their own far away from their native C. Even the trickle of disciples who had once sought out Rabbi Eliyahu's wisdom had slowed and eventually ceased altogether. And so, here he sat, in the middle of a fine day, wondering if the younger Jewish householders in C. were impatient for him finally to move on to the World to Come—as if he was a rude guest in this lowly world who had lingered too long and become a burden to his hosts.

As these grim thoughts swirled about his mind, a stranger, clearly a Jew from his gabardine and beard and *payes*, approached and called out: Rabbi Eliyahu, is that you? I was told at the inn that this is Rabbi Eliyahu's house. I have an urgent message for him from the holy community of the *shtetl* of V.

Startled by this unexpected interruption, Eliyahu answered him: Yes, friend, I am Rabbi Eliyahu. Please, come inside, and we can discuss whatever it is you have traveled all this way to discuss.

Eliyahu rose slowly and painfully; his bones had become so stiff lately. Once he was on his feet, he led the stranger inside to the kitchen and poured two glasses of brandy. After pronouncing the blessing over their liquor, Eliyahu asked the stranger who he was and what was the urgent message.

The stranger did not touch his glass. Trembling slightly, he said: Rabbi Eliyahu, master and teacher, I come to you from the *shtetl* of V. Our holy community is in grave danger. For many generations, we have lived peacefully under our noblemen. But the new *Pan*, Count Jozef P., is different. He is a young man and has no wife. Instead of marrying and settling down in his manor house, like his father and grandfather and all their fathers, he has traveled to faraway cities in Italy, in France, in who knows where else.

A few weeks ago, he returned home. We started to hear strange rumors about him—whispers from his servants when they came down to V. to buy goods for the manor house. During his travels, *Pan* Jozef had purchased a doll who looks exactly like a real woman—face, limbs, hair, lips—everything. He is obsessed with this doll. He spends hours sitting with it, even talking to it. He props it up on couches and chairs. He once laid it down next to him in his bed. He has declared himself to be in love with the doll.

You are probably thinking to yourself: *Nu*, fine, the *goy* nobleman has gone insane and sooner or later one of his relatives will come around and deal with him. But what does this have to do with the Jews of V.?

Oy, on account of our many sins, *Pan* Jozef has gotten it into his crazy head that the doll is a Jew. He found some writing on her forehead or in an amulet around her neck—something like that— and some other nobleman told him the writing was Hebrew. So, he is convinced that his doll is Jewish and that the Jews can bring her to life for him. He has heard legends of kabbalists using magical formulae to create golems out of clay that could walk and talk. He thinks the same *kabbalah* will bring his doll to life.

Pan Jozef summoned the rabbi of V. and the leading householders to his manor house. He calmly explained the situation, showed them the doll, and asked how much time they needed to bring it to life.

The rabbi and the householders did not know what to say. They hemmed and hawed about how such things required a deep learning in the esoteric Torah that few rabbis possess, and certainly none in V. Perhaps, they gently suggested, His Lordship could just appreciate the doll's beauty and workmanship like the other fine statues he owned?

But these sensible words sent *Pan* Jozef into a towering rage. He insisted that the doll was his one and only true love. He could only taste happiness, in this life or the next, in her arms. If his Jews lacked the required mastery of the *kabbalah*, then they must send for another rabbi who could do what had to be done. Should we find him a kabbalist who could bring his beloved doll to life, then no reward would be too great—the synagogue in V would become the grandest in Europe. However, if we should fail him, then he promised to burn our *shul* and our *bet midrash* to the ground.

As you can imagine, we were terrified. While the householders were discussing our dilemma in the *bet midrash* late into the night, a visitor, a merchant traveling on his way to a fair, told us that he had remembered hearing that Rabbi Eliyahu Baal Shem of the *shtetl* of C. had once fashioned a golem out of clay before returning him to the dust. Still, that was so long ago that he was not sure if you were even still alive. We decided to send a messenger—that is, myself—to C. to ask after you or any disciples you might have. And what luck have I found—here you are, the master and teacher, the sage of the *kabbalah*, himself.

So, can you help us?

Eliyahu Baal Shem sighed and drank some brandy. He remembered only too well his adventure with the golem. The creature had seemed a blessing at first—he did the work of ten men and never tired and never slept. But he grew dangerous. And so, Eliyahu had erased the letter *aleph* from the word *Emet* on the golem's forehead, leaving *Met*, death. The golem immediately fell to the ground, lifeless. Eliyahu had then ground his clay body into shards, and ground the shards into dust that he scattered.

He had never tried again to create a golem. Still, he had kept his copy of the secret manuscript of Eleazar of Worms—may the memory of the righteous be for a blessing—that set forth the combinations of holy names and special prayers and rituals for breathing life into a golem. But no—he would not do it again.

Thus, Rabbi Eliyahu Baal Shem answered the messenger from the *shtetl* of V: Friend, I am sorry you have traveled all this way for nothing. It has been many years since I fashioned a golem. I am not sure how much I even remember. But there is a good reason I stopped making golems—they are dangerous.

I would not worry too much about your *Pan*. I have seen many noblemen in my long life. At bottom, they all want the same things: Liquor, women, fat boar meat, heaps of coins and pretty clothes. They are spiritually empty. So, this nobleman has some crazy whim about a doll? It will pass—he is probably just bored, and soon enough he will pack his carriage off to a famous city where some pretty blonde *shikse* with no shame will tempt his eye.

And if he is actually in love with a doll, then his relatives will run to their Gentile courts and have him declared insane so they can grab his lands for themselves.

Do not despair. These dark clouds will drift away.

But the messenger was not deterred. To the contrary, he said: Rabbi Eliyahu, please forgive me if I am denigrating the honor of a sage as great as you, but I fear you do not grasp the danger that we face in V. This is no whim. The nobleman has spurned many offers of marriage from flesh and blood women with large dowries and famous lineages. When the bishop tried to persuade *Pan* Jozef to get rid of the doll, he let loose his hunting dogs to chase the bishop away and maul his flesh.

Nu, do you understand now? This is a matter of life and death. If he is willing to attack the priests of his own church, what would he be willing to do to us? You have made a golem before—you can give him what he wants. And if his doll becomes wicked or dangerous, that will be His Lordship's concern and no one else's. None of us are marrying her. She can torment him, or murder him, for all we care. But for right now, we must soothe the nobleman's wrath before he does something terrible.

Eliyahu felt a cold shiver in his spine listening to these words. If this *Pan* was so far gone in his madness that he would assault a bishop with his hunting dogs, then he would not hesitate to burn down a synagogue, desecrate a Torah scroll, or worse. Necessity breaks iron—and who could say what a lunatic would consider necessary to bring his fantasies to life?

And what was the worst that could happen if he brought the doll to life? That she would be a miserable, browbeating shrew of a wife to the *Pan*? Or beat him, or destroy his property? But what concern was any of that for an old Jewish scholar?

That is, if the doll could even be brought to life. He had never heard of a female golem. Every golem he had heard of, read about, or created with his own hands, had been a man, or a clay imitation of a man. A female golem? Who would fashion such a thing? The kabbalist master who would make a female golem to serve him would have to be so depraved in his sick lusts, so lost under the sway of his evil inclination . . . that . . . that . . . Eliyahu could not even bring himself to imagine it.

So, he told the messenger that he would agree to travel to V. and meet with the nobleman and try to breathe a soul into the doll. He packed up the manuscripts he would need to guide him in animating a golem, as well as a few provisions for the road. Then the two men went to the inn in the *shtetl* of C. where the messenger had left his wagon. They quickly located his coachman, hitched the horses, and departed along the main highway.

Four days later they arrived in the *shtetl* of V.

II. A Cabinet of Curiosities

WHEN THEY ARRIVED in V., the messenger led Eliyahu Baal Shem to the home of the town's rabbi. This rabbi, a scholar named Yitzhak, greeted Eliyahu warmly, and offered him brandy, kugel, and honey cake. Eliyahu happily ate and drank his full, as it had been many hours since their last stop at an inn. When he was done, he said to his host that he had heard from the messenger that the Jews of V. were being persecuted by their mad nobleman.

Rabbi Yitzhak nodded and replied: On account of our many sins, we are being punished. This crazy *Pan* threatens to burn our homes down unless we can satisfy his whims. But our prayers have been answered—for the Holy One, Blessed be He, has sent you to us. Now, tell me, Rabbi Eliyahu Baal Shem, is it true that you know the secret of bringing a golem to life? If the *Pan* presents you with his doll, can you bring her to life?

Eliyahu hesitated slightly and then said: Yes, many years ago I came upon the esoteric manuscripts of Rabbi Eleazar of Worms of blessed memory, and from those manuscripts I learned the secret of breathing a soul into a golem. But I was forced to destroy the one golem I made. Since that time, I have tried not to think too much about golems. Does your nobleman truly believe that his doll is a golem that I could bring to life? Has he gone so mad that he wants a golem for his bride?

Rabbi Yitzhak shook his head sadly and confirmed that the *Pan* had indeed sworn that he had fallen in love with his doll, which he was sure had once been a living golem molded and animated by some learned kabbalist.

Eliyahu continued: Perhaps I can convince him that a golem will make for a poor wife. Every scholar who has ever made a golem destroyed it in the end. For good reason—Creation is best left to the Holy One, Blessed be He. And how can this nobleman even know if his doll was ever a golem? He is no kabbalist. He is not even a Christian priest.

Yitzhak replied: There are faded Hebrew letters on her forehead and the amulet around her neck is also written in Hebrew.

So, Eliyahu asked, what do these Hebrew letters say? Were you able to inspect the amulet?

Yitzhak answered: Yes, I inspected both the amulet and her forehead. The letters were clearly Hebrew. But it was a jumble of nonsense to my eyes. Perhaps it is esoteric Torah wisdom that is beyond my learning. Or maybe it is gibberish—maybe some crazy monk or priest wrote them. You will know the truth of these matters, though, when you see the amulet. As you know the combinations of holy names to craft a golem and breathe a soul into it, you can tell us—tell *him*—if this really is a golem.

And if it is not really a golem, Eliyahu said, what will His Lordship do?

Yitzhak said: Let us pray it is a golem, that you bring it to life, and that he takes his golem bride far away from here. But for tonight, come stay with me. Tomorrow, we will visit *Pan* Jozef and his doll.

Eliyahu Baal Shem slept well that night. The journey had been taxing on his old body, and it was good to rest. The next day Rabbi Yitzhak woke him early, and they went to the synagogue together for their morning prayers. Afterwards, Eliyahu, Yitzhak, and a wealthy householder who leased *Pan* Jozef's vodka distilleries and flour mills piled into the householder's fine carriage and drove off to His Lordship's manor house.

After an hour or so, the carriage halted before an imposing mansion. Eliyahu marveled at the sight of it: Unlike the shabby palaces of the humble gentry near his *shtetl* of C., this was a fortress of stone and marble, three stories high and longer than a city street. In the front of the veranda were tall, rounded columns—just like, Eliyahu mused, there must have been in front of that temple of the Philistines where Samson had been bound and chained.

Upon this porch were a few servants milling about, craning their necks and whispering and pointing at Eliyahu. One of them eventually stepped forward, a stocky, red-faced, robust man with an air of command whom Eliyahu assumed to be the steward of the household. He greeted Rabbi Yitzhak and the wealthy Jewish householder and asked if Eliyahu was the famed kabbalist whom they had promised to bring. When they said yes, he sighed with what sounded to Eliyahu like relief from some grave worry and ushered the three visitors inside.

They passed through a short hallway into a parlor room. Once more, Eliyahu was dazzled by the opulence before his eyes: The furniture was richly upholstered; on the walls hung immense paintings of pretty maidens in immodest dresses being chased by bearded, leering men with goat's horns and feet. And on the blue-veined marble mantelpiece sat a group of carefully arranged tiny stuffed birds whose feathers were a riot of wild, bright colors.

The steward told them to have a seat and then left for roughly a quarter of an hour. When he returned, he was accompanied by an elegantly dressed, strikingly handsome young man beaming with pleasure. He and the steward quickly exchanged words in a language that Eliyahu did not understand. The young man then addressed

himself to Eliyahu in the same incomprehensible babble. At this
point, the wealthy householder intervened.

In response, the young man addressed himself to Eliyahu in
Yiddish, and thus his words finally made sense: My apologies, Rabbi,
for speaking in Polish. My dear friend and leaseholder here, Reb
Mendel, informs me that your people's scholars are not well
acquainted with the tongues of your Christian neighbors. But I
believe my Yiddish will be adequate to our task so long as you are
careful not to slip any flowery Hebrew phrases into your remarks.

Now, for a proper introduction: I am Count Jozef P., lord of
this estate, including the market town of V., where, through my
generosity, I have permitted a community of Jews to reside and
practice their faith in peace and security—peace and security that I
have personally guaranteed. In exchange for my liberality and
protection, I expect my Jewish subjects to provide me with certain
items that I may require from time to time. And what I require at
the moment is a rabbi expert in the formulae and rituals necessary
for the animation of an object fashioned of clay. Tell me, Rabbi, do
you have the knowledge I seek?

Eliyahu straightened his hoary, bent back as well as he could,
cleared his throat, and answered: Your Honor, it is a privilege to be
received by such a great and mighty lord—a privilege I am in no way
worthy of. My name is Eliyahu Baal Shem, from the *shtetl* of C. I am
a scholar learned in the *kabbalah* and I have fashioned and brought
life to a golem.

Pan Jozef nodded in response and signaled to Eliyahu to follow
him, although he told Yitzhak and Mendel to remain where they
were in the parlor. The two men exited and turned into a winding,
dimly lit hallway and eventually arrived in a room that, although
spacious and well lit, appeared to Eliyahu to be the refuse heap of a
lunatic: Everywhere around him were animal skeletons, pelts,
misshapen rocks, broken shards of pottery, tiny statues, rusted coins
that did not resemble any currency that Eliyahu had ever seen, and

bizarre paintings not resembling any person or place that Eliyahu could recognize.

Pan Jozef, however, glowed with pride before all this clutter. He said: Rabbi, I welcome you to my Cabinet of Curiosities. All the genuinely civilized noble lords of Europe, friends of the international Republic of Letters and devotees of natural philosophy, maintain such collections in their homes. I have traveled far and wide to assemble these objects. Here, we may examine the vertebrae of unusual birds and beasts from the New World and Africa; rare minerals from islands in the remote Pacific; the artifacts of ancient empires in Europe and China; and miniature paintings from the courts of the Mughal kings of India. And yet this magnificent gallery is but a small, modest part of the march of progress and the advancement of knowledge that has lit the fires of enlightenment in all the capitals of Europe.

Rabbi Eliyahu quietly nodded along so as not to upset the young lord. But he mused to himself: Truth and knowledge were to be found within the words of the Holy One, Blessed be He, as passed down through the written and oral Torah and the teachings of the sages of blessed memory. What could a rock or a skeleton, the flotsam and jetsam of *HaShem*'s divine and perfect Creation, possibly teach that the holy and perfect words of the Torah could not?

Still, he had to humor this fool and be patient with him.

Pan Jozef continued: But I have not brought you here to discourse upon the discoveries made by gentlemen learned in science and reason. I recognize that you are an old cleric lost in the cobwebs of centuries of superstition. However, I also recognize that certain of your superstitions may contain genuine kernels of knowledge. Before Newton revealed the workings of the universe with mathematical precision, ancient astrologers divined the future through star charts. Yet beneath their superstitions, they were at times able to intuit some aspects of the natural laws that Newton later discovered. I think there may be something similar in your *kabbalah*—that beneath the accreted layers of silly childish fables, your people may have learned how to access and manipulate the workings of natural laws that still await their Newton to unravel and make them plain. Indeed, I am a member of a fraternal order, a secret society, of like-minded gentlemen of learning and enlightenment, who seek to discover the scientific underpinnings behind ancient rites of magic and divination, and the occult practices of the Egyptian priests, Persian magi, and Greek adepts.

Which brings me to the reason I have brought you here. There is another object in my Cabinet of Curiosities, which is not merely a finely crafted article to be displayed and studied. To the contrary, it is alive. Yet it is a living thing whose life has been somehow snuffed out and must be restored.

I should correct myself: It is not a thing. It is a woman. The most beautiful, tender, and exquisite of women—a lady whose natural, ingenuous charm puts to shame the legions of cold, scheming coquettes, with their painted faces and affected manners, who tease and torment the gentlemen of Warsaw and Vienna and Paris. She is an innocent, pure child of nature, who has not been corrupted by our modern civilization and its decadent morals.

The young *Pan* then signaled for Eliyahu to follow him into a small room off to the side. It was cramped—more a nook or a closet than a room—and lit only by a slender lamp hanging from the ceiling. Inside this alcove was a large glass case holding a strikingly lifelike doll of a young woman with thick black hair. Her skin was coarse and had a dull orange tint to it. She was dressed modestly, and her expression was almost bashful, like a pious daughter of Israel ashamed to find herself alone with two strange men gazing at her. An object hung about her neck and there were faint markings on her forehead. But because she was resting on a tall pedestal that elevated her well above the ground, Eliyahu could not make out what was written on her face.

Pan Jozef spoke again: Rabbi, this woman standing before you is my beloved. While she may lack nobility of birth, she has nobility of spirit, a nobility far rarer and more precious. You can see her natural humility and her caring heart. But her animating soul has been snatched away or rendered inert.

I am sure I sound like a madman to you, devoting my affections to a doll made of earthenware and clay. Yet from the many hours I have spent staring into her eyes, I know that she is alive, full of love and tenderness. She is a princess frozen in a living death, and I am the prince who must awaken her.

However, when I pressed my lips against hers, nothing happened. I showed her to my brothers in that certain secret society whose name I dare not utter aloud. These gentlemen are learned and wise philosophers who have studied the occult sciences and the ancient traditions of Hermes Trismegistus. But, nonetheless, their efforts to penetrate the mystery of the doll proved unavailing. Still, when they examined the amulet around her neck, they immediately recognized the writing as Hebrew. Although they could decipher a phrase here or there, the text as a whole was inscrutable to them. I realized that I needed a scholar with an expertise in esoteric Jewish lore far beyond theirs.

In order to ensure that I secured the services of a rabbi with the requisite capabilities, I asked my secret brothers to tell me about any Jewish practices or books that could aid me. That is when they told me about the various tales they had heard of rabbinical adepts molding men out of clay and breathing life into them. The rabbis who practiced this dark art referred to their resulting creations as golems. However, none of them knew of any actual golems alive in Europe at the moment, or of any recent attempts to fashion one.

Hence, I turned to my Jewish subjects. They, too, pleaded ignorance. But I would not be put off by their excuses, and I insisted that they bring to me a rabbi with enough learning in the occult sciences of the Jews to bring my beloved back to life. I am convinced that she was once a golem, molded and animated by a powerful kabbalist sorcerer who sought to create a woman more natural, innocent, and tender than the corrupt, venal, lying creatures that pass for the female of our species today.

Tell me, Rabbi, can you bring my beloved back to life?

By this point, Eliyahu Baal Shem was certain that the nobleman had gone mad. Why would he think that his doll had ever been a golem? Dolls are dolls and statues are statues and they are all empty dead idols. A golem was quite rare—the clay figure must be fashioned correctly from just the right material, and even then, it took immense knowledge and spiritual strength to draw down an animating soul from the divine flux of the *Ein Sof*, the Infinite and Perfect Godhead. Still, this *Pan* Jozef needed to be humored.

So, Eliyahu answered His Lordship: Your Honor, it is no small matter to speak of a golem. A carpenter can shape a piece of wood into the likeness of a person. If the carpenter is expert in his trade, that likeness can seem so real that you feel as if the wooden statue is looking into your eyes like an actual person. But it is an illusion—a trick—because there is no person there.

Our holy sages—may the memory of the righteous be for a blessing—taught that when Our Father Abraham was a child, his father owned a shop that sold idols. One day, little Abraham was left in charge of the shop. A woman came in with a plate of food to offer to the idols. Abraham thanked her, took the food, and then smashed all the idols except the biggest one. Next to this biggest one he placed a large stick.

Later that day, his father returned to the store and demanded to know what had happened to all his merchandise—how were all of the idols but one shattered into tiny bits? And Abraham said: A woman offered food to the idols, but they fought with each other over who would get to eat it. So, the biggest idol grabbed a stick and killed all the others. But his father replied: You idiot! These statues cannot think or move by themselves.

And that is the way of statues and dolls and idols fashioned by mortal men out of wood and stone and whatever else may be at hand. These things may look like men, but they have no soul. It is for the Holy One, Blessed be He, alone to breathe life into a figure made of dirt and clay, as He did with Adam.

Nevertheless, it is possible, for those who are pious and learned in the *kabbalah*, to fashion a clay figure in a very particular manner from very particular materials, and then to engage in difficult spiritual exercises and ascents of the soul to reach the Throne of Glory and draw down the divine life force that births souls into being. Such is how golems are made.

I did this once, many years ago. And then my golem grew threatening, dangerous. I killed him, although he nearly killed me first. There are few scholars with the learning and piety to fashion a golem, and even fewer still who would actually want to create one.

So, Your Honor, you can understand that I may be skeptical that your doll was actually once a golem fashioned by a scholar of the *kabbalah*. But if you would permit me to inspect the Hebrew amulet around her neck, perhaps matters will become clearer.

Pan Jozef said nothing in response, but left briefly to grab a stool from the next room, which he then placed in front of the glass case holding the doll. After mounting its steps, he pulled a key from his pocket, unlocked the case, and gently, almost tenderly, removed the amulet from around the doll's neck. Before coming back down, he leaned in closely to the doll and whispered into her ear and caressed her neck and breasts.

While the nobleman was taking his strange liberties with the doll, Eliyahu Baal Shem felt the doll's eyes were looking down at him—no, more than that, they were piercing into his flesh. They seemed to be full of suffering, as if she were pleading with him— Rabbi Eliyahu—for help. But no—this was crazy. She was a statue, an idol—dirt and clay and paint. He averted his eyes and stared at the floor, although he still felt the weight of her gaze.

Eventually, *Pan* Jozef finished doing whatever he was doing with his doll, closed the case, came back down again, and handed the amulet to Eliyahu Baal Shem. The parchment was old and faded and even blotted out in a few places, but Eliyahu could still read it. The letters and words were certainly Hebrew. As he read on, Eliyahu felt a heavy pit growing in his stomach, for these Hebrew words formed no simple blessings. No, these were combinations of esoteric, hidden true names for the Holy One, Blessed be He—names that could be used to wield great power by a scholar with the right knowledge and pious concentration.

The holy names, and their particular order and permutations, seemed eerily familiar. He had read something similar, if not identical, quite recently. But what was it? This was not from any of the famous commentaries. It was something else—something few had ever seen, something usually concealed.

And then he remembered: The amulet in his hands was a copy of a portion of the manuscript of Eleazar of Worms setting forth the steps and incantations for fashioning a golem and drawing a soul down into its body. This was the same manuscript that Eliyahu Baal Shem himself had once used to make his own golem. The mad nobleman might actually be right—his doll could have been a golem—could have been, that is, if this amulet had originally belonged with her and was placed around her neck by her creator.

Eliyahu turned back to *Pan* Jozef and asked, with a newfound sharpness in his tone: How did you come to acquire this amulet? Why do you believe it relates to this doll?

But His Lordship answered a question with a question: Why, rabbi, the sudden interest in the amulet? What do those Hebrew words say, exactly? Tell me.

Eliyahu sighed with irritation and replied: The meaning of the words is beyond your understanding. I would not dare to utter them aloud, even if you should threaten me with torture or death, for they are too holy and terrible. The meaning of this amulet can only be grasped after many years of study of the *kabbalah*.

Does it at least relate to our subject of golems? the nobleman asked.

Eliyahu did not respond. He did not wish to lie, but he was hesitant to reveal the truth. He did not relish the thought of bringing another golem to life. And he assumed that whatever scholar had created this doll woman golem had also taken away her soul for good reason.

His worried thoughts must have seeped from his mind into his countenance because *Pan* Jozef suddenly said: Rabbi, from your grave expression, it is clear that this amulet is a secret charm, or perhaps a kabbalistic grimoire, for making a golem. Now you have both the proof that she is a golem and the magical formulae you will need for her soul's resurrection, or perhaps restoration.

Eliyahu, however, replied that he was still unsure that the Hebrew amulet related to this doll. How did His Honor know they were connected? How had he acquired these objects?

Pan Jozef frowned, but then his expression relaxed and he said: While I should take offense at some greasy *żhyd* questioning my word, I understand that the matter of animating a golem implicates a science beyond my ken and into which only a tiny handful of rabbis like yourself have been initiated. There may, perhaps, be subtle details and nuances that I have glossed over that could be important for our task. Follow me to my library room where we can sit comfortably. We will rest, and I will tell you the tale of how I came to acquire this doll and her amulet.

III. A Curiosity in a Cabinet

ONCE THEY WERE both seated in opposite facing, comfortably cushioned chairs in the library, *Pan* Jozef launched into his tale: I had been traveling in Italy for some time. In Venice, I had made contact with other members of my secret brotherhood. We exchanged manuscripts and shared discoveries regarding the occult and forbidden sciences, and I inspected their collections of specimens and artifacts. I did not wish to return to Poland, and I even considered attempting, through the good offices of an Italian nobleman of my acquaintance, to secure some perch in Italian society—perhaps as the representative of the Polish crown at the court of some petty duke. But, to my dismay, I received a letter from my father summoning me home, as I had—in his opinion—lingered long enough amusing myself in foreign climes and spent far too much money. Back home, he commanded, I would need to seek a wealthy bride. And so, with a heavy sigh and many heartfelt farewells to my secret brothers, I departed Italy and all its beauty and wonders.

I slowly made my way north and east towards Poland. I was in no hurry to return to my father and his demands that I marry. Marriage—I could imagine it in my mind: A wife and a litter of toddlers screeching at me. They would have no regard for my cabinet of curiosities, so lovingly and carefully curated. They would break my pottery and my statues. My wife, like all women, would endeavor to remake our home in her own tiresomely vulgar image—and she would no doubt exile my researches to a tiny corner of the cellar, where she and her feminine guests would not have to endure them. Yet however wretched was the prospect of marriage, without my own independent fortune, I had little choice but to submit to my father's will.

My father grew impatient with my slow pace of travel. He dispatched ever angrier letters demanding that I proceed more quickly, threatening to slash my funds to the bare minimum necessary for the journey. Casting about for an excuse to continue delaying my homecoming, I remembered that my late mother had a cousin who lived on an estate in the Carpathian Mountains in Hungary. Thus, I wrote to my father that I intended to visit this relative, whom I had never met. I noted that it would be an unpardonable breach of etiquette and a stain on my honor were I to pass by without paying my respects as a kinsman. My father was irritated, but he could not disagree—calling upon my cousin *was* the honorable and courteous thing for a young man to do.

My coach turned away from the direct road home and swerved deep into the mountains. I spent several days in miserable travel through impoverished lands: neglected roads overrun with weeds and mud, peasants reeking of animal manure and worse, and screaming curses in some bizarre incomprehensible language. And the inns—suffice to say, my flesh was a banquet for the many hungry insects that made their abodes in those mattresses.

Eventually, I arrived at my cousin's estate. He lived in a castle halfway up a grey, lifeless mountain dotted with stunted trees. The castle appeared to have once been a mighty fort left to slide into disrepair. Still, inside the walls there was a lovely, if small, family chapel and my cousin's residence had been adequately, if not lavishly, maintained.

I had sent word ahead to my cousin that I intended to pay him a visit, so that when I at last arrived, I received a warm and joyous welcome. I ate decent food that night for the first time since I had detoured into those wretched mountains, and the wine was exquisite. My bed was mercifully free from insects and as soft and comfortable as I could have wished.

The next morning, my cousin rode with me through the countryside and showed me his vineyards, the source of that wonderful wine. I discovered that he too was a man of enlightenment and reason. We spoke at length of scientific enquiries and antiquarian investigations.

When we returned to the castle in the late afternoon he showed me his library, which held many volumes of both the ancients and the moderns. Directly behind the library was another room, which housed his cabinet of curiosities. The contents were not exotic or far flung—nothing from Asia or the New World, not even anything from Italy or Greece. Instead, he had gathered specimens of locally mined minerals and the skeletons of a bear and a wolf, probably felled by his peasants. There were some intriguing remains of ancient weapons and armor that my cousin had uncovered on his estate, which he insisted were relics from the army of Attila the Hun.

Amidst these various objects, I noticed a tall glass case in the corner. Inside this case was a life-size doll of a beautiful maiden who seemed almost alive—the very doll that you have now seen in my home. And around her neck hung the same Hebrew amulet that you were just inspecting.

I asked my cousin where he had acquired such a striking replica of a woman—the most lifelike doll or statue I had ever beheld. Rather than answer me, he walked over to the glass case, fell to his knees, and looked up at the doll with an expression of heartrending tenderness in his eyes. He sat there on his knees, staring and silent, for several minutes. Then he burst into tears and mumbled something under his breath that I could not hear clearly.

Once he had recovered himself, he led me back to his library. I was eager to learn what about that doll had so unsettled my cousin's otherwise sound mind. For up until that moment, he had been a perfect exemplar of an enlightened gentleman, witty, learned, and even-tempered. Yet before this doll he had suddenly collapsed into some mad ecstasy like a superstitious monk in a dank cell having visions of the devil. Still, I did not wish to upset my host or abuse his hospitality, so I held my tongue and waited—hoped—that he would choose to share the causes of his anguish with me.

We sat together in silence for a long time. My cousin sighed often and wiped stray tears from his cheek. There was a carafe of wine on the table wedged between our chairs, from which he poured out generous libations for himself. I also sipped the fine wine and watched the sun set over the mountain peaks through the window opposite me.

After darkness had fallen, my cousin at last spoke. He told me that many years ago, when he was a young man, he had been traveling through a forest when a great storm suddenly arose without warning. A lightning bolt struck a tree, which in turn fell on his carriage. The horses fled in terror, and the coachman was knocked to the ground, instantly killed. My cousin was now alone amidst the rain, wind, and thunder. He sheltered as best he could beneath the wreck of the coach for the duration of the storm and prayed desperately for a safe homecoming.

Once the weather had turned mild again, he slithered out from underneath his broken carriage. His leg was badly hurt, and he was forced to limp. He also had caught a chill in his lungs, and he coughed and shivered continually. As he walked down the forest road, ankle deep in the thick mud, he grew feverish and delirious. He stumbled over to a tree, and sat down against its trunk. He was sure his life would shortly reach its end: If the sickness did not finish him off, then some wild beast would. Full of despair, he drifted off to sleep.

When he awoke again, he was lying in a warm bed inside an unfamiliar house. His wet clothes were gone, and he was wearing a soft, dry robe. For a moment he thought he had passed to the next world, but then he felt a sharp pain in his leg, and he knew that his soul was still firmly planted inside his body.

He called out and asked if anyone was there.

In response, two persons entered the room. One was an old Jewish man with kind eyes and a long beard. Next to him was a beautiful maiden whom he introduced as his daughter. The old man said they had found my cousin lying unconscious in the forest, with his teeth chattering and sweat pouring down his forehead, and they had taken him back to their house to nurse him back to health. The old man was quite pleased to see my cousin awake and told his daughter to fetch a pot of tea and some bread and preserves.

My cousin spent several weeks recuperating in that old Jew's house. The daughter did much of the work of looking after him—cooking for him, washing his body, helping him to stand up again and then later to walk. This maiden was not only beautiful in body, but also in spirit. She was bashful and modest, so unlike the coquettish vultures whom my cousin had met in the salons of Europe's better society. She would blush and stammer at the slightest compliment. And although she dressed plainly, she carried herself with grace and dignity.

My cousin fell deeply in love. He proposed marriage to her, and promised to take her away from her forest dwelling to live with him in his castle and vineyards. He swore that he would devote his days only to her happiness.

In reply, she asked what would become of her frail, aged father if she left him alone in the woods, with no one to care for him?

My cousin offered that her father could live with them too. He would be cared for by the many servants in his household.

Still, she hesitated. She said she would need time to ponder such a weighty matter. She had to consider as well the question of her faith. She could not marry a Christian and remain a Jew. And it would break her father's heart for her to accept baptism.

The pure, lovely maiden asked for six months to consider the proposal. In the meantime, she urged her suitor to return to his estate and put his affairs in order. She said that, if she were to marry him, she did not want to enter a castle in disarray.

Heeding her advice, my cousin departed from the kindly pair in the forest and returned to his castle. With his heart bursting with hope, he was a whirlwind of activity—reconciling ledgers and accounts, satisfying debts, inspecting his vineyards and wine presses and ordering many improvements to each, and even hiring craftsmen to repair each crack in the walls or rip in the furniture.

Nevertheless, despite the distractions of this frenzy of work, my cousin yearned continually to be reunited with his love. He dreamed of her each night, and wrote silly but sincere verses about his undying devotion to his Fairy Nymph Jewess of the Woods.

When the six months' wait at last ended, my cousin outfitted a splendid carriage and returned to the same forest with an impressive entourage of valets, footmen, guards, and huntsmen. Happiness was now within his grasp—he could already feel himself nestling against his beloved by the hearth on dark, cold winter nights, sipping cocoa together and listening to the howling of the wind.

But then, to his surprise and dismay, he could not find the house in the forest again. They searched for weeks, scouring every path and clearing. They questioned the local peasants, but none of them had ever heard of two Jews, a father and a daughter, living together in a house in the woods. Eventually, my cousin returned home, heartbroken, with his sweetest hopes dissolved to dust.

His robust constitution and enthusiastic labors vanished along with his dreams of wedded bliss. Now he could barely lift himself out of bed. And when he did arise, often late in the morning, he would wander aimlessly about in his nightclothes. He was perpetually irritable and berated any servant unlucky enough to cross his path. At times, he would sit by a window, gazing outside and weeping for hours. He saw no one, and lost all interest in his affairs and the management of his estate. Eating little, he grew thin and sickly. Rumors swirled that he would die soon, unmarried, childless, and without an heir. The vultures began to circle, laying the groundwork to make a legal claim to his lands after what was assumed to be his imminent demise.

But not everyone had lost hope. His neighboring landowners—perhaps fearing which distant relation might succeed to the estate—banded together and settled on a bride to press upon my cousin, as they had heard he was wasting away from a broken heart. The cure, they were sure, was a wife. And not just any wife: To rescue him from such an all-consuming melancholy, the bride must be so beautiful and charming as to make any other maiden pale in comparison.

The young lady they settled upon, the nineteen-year-old daughter of a minor noble who had gambled away his patrimony, was indeed ravishingly beautiful and gifted in all the civilized and feminine arts. They brought her to my gloomy cousin—dangled her like a shiny piece of bait on the end of a fishing rod.

And their scheme was a success: Her charms brought him out of his grief and back into, if not exactly joy, then at least a tolerably normal state of health. He married the lovely maiden, and they had a few children in quick succession.

But he was not a man fated to know happiness. All the children were taken by illness. His wife grew restless. She took lovers and traveled abroad without her husband for months at a time. My cousin seethed in his humiliation yet felt helpless against her cunning words—in every argument, somehow the adulteress made herself appear to be the aggrieved victim of her husband's boorishness and jealousy. But in time, she too perished: She lingered a little too long in the arms of a lover in Naples, and the unhealthy hot summer air penetrated her lungs and she fell ill and died.

Once again alone, my cousin decided to embark on a journey of his own. He hoped that a change in scenery—new sensations and stimuli for his nerves—would boost his spirits. My cousin set out for Vienna, where he stayed for several weeks.

One day at dusk, towards the end of his visit, he came upon a brightly lit shop. The proprietor noticed that a gentleman had stopped in front of his window, and he invited my cousin inside to sample his merchandise. This store could be best described as a shop of curiosities. It was a mess of animal skeletons, insects from the New World preserved and mounted in cases, shards of ancient pottery and statues, discarded reliquary boxes, and much more of the like.

Amidst this clutter, however, my cousin came upon a tall glass case in the back. He fell to his knees before it, and his heart pounded so terribly that he thought it might leap out of his chest. For inside the glass case was a perfectly lifelike doll of a young woman who was identical in every particular to his long-lost true love, his Fairy Nymph Jewess of the Woods. He wept and begged her forgiveness for marrying another.

He immediately purchased the glass case and the doll, and had them brought back to his castle. After she was installed in his cabinet of curiosities, he would spend hours gazing upon her, speaking to her, laughing with her, and reciting the sentimental verses he had written about her so many years ago. Even though she appeared to be a doll, he felt certain that she was alive—that her soul was trapped inside the figurine and he had but to coax it out in order to at last, after so much suffering, taste true happiness and true love.

Thus was my cousin's tale. I thought he had gone mad from all his grief. But then I too began to sit at the feet of the doll. I too felt the soft caresses of her eyes—could feel that spirit, so full of tenderness and innocence, bathe me in its light. The longer I sat at her feet and gazed upon her, the deeper grew my love. I lost interest in other pursuits, and declined every invitation to ride or hunt or peruse some rare volume in my cousin's library.

My cousin grew suspicious, or jealous, or perhaps both. He ordered the room with the doll to be bolted and shut, and directed his servants to deny me entry. He also suggested that it might be time for me to resume my journey home to my father.

I fell into despair. Without the reassuring and tender gaze of the doll, I lost the will to rise from my bed in the morning. I refused almost all food, and subsisted for a time on tea and bread. I pondered climbing to the highest rampart and hurling myself down the side of the mountain.

But then my despair turned to rage. Who was my cousin to claim exclusive possession of her? By his own admission, he had encountered her in the forest when she was still animate, and he had let her go. Or else he had failed in his attempts to persuade her to leave with him. Either way, he had shown himself to be unworthy of her love. And now he was holding her prisoner for his amusement. She deserved a better fate. What kind of lover was I if I could be deterred by so petty an obstacle as a lock on the door? She had gazed upon me with such longing, such devotion. It was plainly her wish to leave my cousin and be with me—what else could explain her pleading stares?

I would not fail my beloved in her hour of need. I gave my coachman orders to ready the horses and carriage for a midnight departure, but to tell no one of our plans. Meanwhile, to throw off my cousin's suspicions, I ate a hearty breakfast, and spent the day riding about his estates and sampling the barrels at his wine press. I even pretended to pay court to a pretty peasant girl. By evening time, he was doubtless convinced that I had lost interest in his doll.

I feigned sleep and waited until I could be sure that everyone else had retired to bed. Then I rose from beneath my blankets and donned slippers that muffled the sound of my steps. I crept into my cousin's room as he snored merrily, and made off with the key to that most precious room of his. From there, it was an easy task to remove the glass case and convey it to my carriage. I say now it was an easy task but, upon reflection, the case must have been quite heavy and difficult to grasp. Such is the power of true, genuine passion—it lightens the heaviest of burdens.

My coachman took off as soon as I and the doll were ensconced in the rear compartment. We rode without stopping until we had left my cousin's lands and the miserable Carpathian villages and reached a city with a respectable inn where we could eat and rest. There, I posted a letter to my father and requested him to write back to me at the next stopping point on our itinerary.

When we reached that city three weeks later, I found a letter waiting for me. But it was not from my father. Instead, the steward of our estates wrote to regretfully inform me of two deaths. The first was my father. While he had been hunting, something startled his horse, the beast threw him off, and he fell against a sharp rock that fractured his skull. His huntsmen managed to get him back to his bed in his manor house, but their efforts to staunch the bleeding were of no avail and he did not last the night.

The other death was my cousin, the one from whom I had rescued my beloved, the doll. In the days after my sudden departure, he sank into such a deep melancholy that he would not stir from his bed. If anyone tried to lift his spirits through friendly conversation, he would burst into frenzied, screeching sobs. Then one night, he rose from his bed and mounted the steps to the castle wall. He walked around the ramparts until he reached the spot at which the sheer drop down the mountainside was steepest. From there, he jumped to his death.

The steward concluded by informing me that, as a consequence of these two unexpected and tragic deaths, I had inherited both my father's and my cousin's lands and titles. He looked forward to accompanying me on an inspection of my new estates and their record books, as well as escorting me to the mausoleum next to the family chapel, where I could pay my respects to my deceased father and offer suitable prayers for the salvation of his immortal soul.

Before receiving that letter, I had feared two things—my father's insistence that I marry, and my cousin's wrath for having taken his beloved. Yet I had been miraculously delivered from both. As I have told you, Rabbi Eliyahu, I am not a superstitious fanatic like you and the other rabbis and priests and clerical parasites. To the contrary, I am a man of enlightenment and science. But how can science explain such an astounding coincidence? If I had read it in a French novel, I would have laughed at the ridiculousness of such a plot contrivance.

I recalled, however, my many discussions with my brothers in our secret society, and how we speculated that, despite the discoveries of Copernicus and Newton, our science may still be so primitive as to fail to grasp many of the subtler laws of nature. My brothers had long studied the occult wisdom and magic of the ancients and the alchemists, seeking to uncover the natural laws that undergirded the apparent wonders and miracles that had awed so many gullible minds.

And then my thoughts turned back to the doll. She was a being whose nature pushed the bounds of our limited knowledge, as she was both inanimate and yet clearly also alive—every time I gazed upon her, I could feel her warm, tender soul enveloping mine. Could *she* have somehow contrived to influence events in my favor? I had certainly confessed to her, during our long carriage rides, my hopes and fears for our future. Did she, as a different and perhaps more exalted being, have the capability of manipulating particular energies in the universe? Could these tragedies be in fact a sign she loved me as I desperately as I loved her, and she was doing all that was in her power to bring our love to fruition?

When we arrived at what was now my estate, I installed my beloved in the room that you visited earlier today. Since then, I have spent hours sitting with her, staring at her, speaking to her. With each passing minute in her presence, I have grown ever more entranced. I wrote to my brothers and urged them to come and inspect her too. They were the ones who identified the amulet's language as Hebrew and recounted the legends of rabbis creating golems from clay and dirt and bringing them to life.

Thus, I sought the aid of my Jewish subjects, who have in turn brought you, Rabbi Eliyahu, to my threshold. Well then, you have inspected the amulet. You have heard all that I know of the wonders of the doll. Tell me—is she indeed a golem? Can you bring her back to life? Should you bring her back to life so that we may be married and live as husband and wife in both body and spirit, two souls united as one, then the synagogues in my towns shall be grander than cathedrals, and I shall work tirelessly to stamp out all traces of those vile ancient prejudices against your Israelite nation.

IV. A Cautionary Tale of Golems Past

RABBI ELIYAHU REFLECTED: From the amulet, it was clear that this doll had once been a golem. The fact that all these *goyim* could sense something alive in her gaze could be a sign that the soul that her maker had drawn down from the higher worlds still remained within her. Or perhaps it was a residue of that soul—maybe just the animal part of the soul and not the higher components? It was hard to say.

Still, he could bring her back to life, with the appropriate preparation and prayers and ascent of his soul. But did this *Pan* Jozef appreciate the dangers of such a thing? If the golem became violent, would he blame the Jews for bringing a plague down upon his house? For now, he spoke of building synagogues like cathedrals, but he could quickly change his mind if the golem turned out not to be such a gentle creature.

Weighing these matters in his mind, Eliyahu Baal Shem decided to give one last warning. And so, he said: Your Honor, it is true that the doll may be a golem. I did not believe you at first, but then I read the divine and secret holy names in the amulet about her neck—when recited with the correct *kavanah*, or spiritual intention, after the proper preparation, and in combination with certain other secret names, the text of that amulet could breathe life into a golem. And if that is truly your wish, I will do so.

But first, please humor an old man for a few minutes. We old men never tire of telling our stories, and I have one about a golem—a golem that I once fashioned and into whose clay body I drew down a soul. When I was a much younger man, I used to wonder about the making of golems. A man can make figures out of clay, and they can appear lifelike, as if they were real people. Yet true creation involved not just forming a body, but also breathing a soul into it so that the creature could live—walk, talk, perhaps even reason. This is why the Holy One, Blessed be He, is so much greater than puny, flimsy mortal men. A good craftsman could, just like *HaShem* did with Adam, form dust and clay into the likeness of a man. However, only *HaShem* could breathe a human soul into that body, a soul that could think and reason, pray and repent and love. Idols were false gods for this very reason: They were figures crafted by men—men who lacked the divine power to bring a statue or a doll to life, to imbue it with a soul.

Nevertheless, I had heard whispered tales of mighty kabbalists creating golems—that is, bringing a clay statue to life by giving it a soul. How could this be? Even to think such a thought—an idol brought to life by human means—was to offend against the Majesty and Oneness of His Name. After all, the Holy One, Blessed be He, had cursed mankind for the sin of building a Tower of Babel soaring into His abode in the Heavenly firmament—and this was an even worse affront to His Torah.

On the other hand, the men who had fashioned golems and brought them to life were not reviled heretics, but rather, each and every one, esteemed sages and scholars.

Tormented by this paradox, I studied the sacred texts and commentaries in search of an explanation. In the beginning, I could find no answers to my questions. But then I had a stroke of luck. I received a letter that a distant relation—a great-uncle—had recently passed on to the next world, may his memory be for a blessing. This great-uncle of mine, whom I barely knew—I may have met him once or twice as a little boy—had owned a large library. In his will, he specified that the scholars in his family—a list that included me—should be invited to examine his books and manuscripts and choose which ones they wished to keep for themselves. Whatever was left would then go to the town's *bet midrash*.

On the appointed day, I inspected his library. In a dusty, far corner of the room, I found a chest filled with manuscripts. And amongst these manuscripts I found a carefully copied treatise from Rabbi Eleazar of Worms, may the memory of the righteous be for a blessing. Skimming his words, I saw that Rabbi Eleazar had recorded the combinations of holy names and the rituals for creating a golem. This was what I had been seeking—an explanation of how the learned sages, pious men whose souls were filled with love for the Torah, had brought clay idols to life.

I claimed Eleazar's treatise as my inheritance from my great-uncle's library and returned home as quickly as I could. Once I was back in my own room, with no distractions, I stayed up the entire night studying it. What Rabbi Eleazar had taught was that the Holy One had used the Hebrew language to draw down the divine flux of life into a soul and then to place that soul into Adam's inert dirt body. This act of creation could be imitated by a scholar invoking certain secret, potent names of the Holy One, Blessed be He. Such a scholar must first use these names to make an ascent of his soul to the *Ein Sof*, the Infinite Source of All, and then bring back the divine sparks from which Creation flows, drawing down a new soul that can be placed within the clay golem's body.

I marveled at what I had read. It seemed so presumptuous as to be sinful—and yet it was not. The Holy One had created us in His image and endowed us with the powers of reason and speech—powers that He had denied to the beasts and the fish and the birds. Perhaps He had intended for us, or at least the pious and learned among us, to use that faculty of speech to harness the power of Creation, a power that flowed through the sacred words of the Hebrew language?

I resolved to fashion a golem according to Rabbi Eleazar's teachings. I told myself this was an act that would bring me closer to the Holy One, Blessed be He—that by partaking in the creation of a being with a soul, I was joining my soul with His Infinite Spirit, a drop of water falling into His endless ocean. But I was an arrogant fool. Puffed up with pride, I wanted to feel the power of being able to create life, and I wanted to prove that I was a mighty enough kabbalist and sage to fashion a golem.

I gathered clay from the bank of a small river near my home. Over the course of several weeks, I molded the clay into the likeness of a living man. Once my clay doll was ready, I spent a week in fasting, prayer, and atonement. I wore white robes and immersed myself in the bath at the *mikveh* each day.

After I had purified myself, I removed my clay doll from its hiding place in the cellar and brought it to the forest. I concentrated upon the combinations of holy and secret names that Rabbi Eleazar had recorded in his commentary. I felt my soul depart from my body and rise up to the heavenly firmament. As I ascended, I encountered many gates that I unlocked through different combinations and repetitions of the letters of the sacred names.

Eventually, my soul came to rest next to a marble fountain in a clearing in an orchard. From the mouth of this fountain poured a light that was like no earthly light. I bathed myself in this light, and I drank of it, and I let it penetrate within me and flow through all my veins. When I was full to the brim, I drifted back downward. I passed again through the same gates, which this time opened for me of their own accord, and then I fell below the firmament and back into my body.

My flesh, though, felt as if it were about to burst apart. My puny body—which was but dust born from a putrid drop—could not contain the holy light from the *Ein Sof.* I was terrified that my allotted days had run their course, and that I had, in my foolishness, doomed myself to an early grave.

Nevertheless, I beheld the clay doll at my feet and remembered my task. I carved the Hebrew word *Emet*—Truth—on his forehead. Then I opened my mouth and spewed out the divine sparks teeming within me. Those sparks, in turn, poured into the clay doll through the Hebrew letters written on his forehead.

Once the heavenly light had left me, I collapsed into a stupor. When I awoke again, the sun was rising and I was lying next to a strange looking man. This was my golem, brought to life. Not that he was much to look at: I had used only so much clay, and had only so much patience in molding it, so my golem was short, narrow, and hairless from his bald head to his toes.

I greeted him, but he did not reply. I stood up. He imitated me and stood up too. I made a gesture that he should follow me, but he did not seem to understand. Still, when I started to walk along on the forest path, he followed me.

And so it went for those first few weeks: He had no speech and little understanding, but he would follow me about and imitate whatever I did. Needless to say, he was no help to me—more of a nuisance. However, then something unexpected came to pass: The golem began to speak. And while the creature was never going to be a scholar, its speech was not too different from a water carrier or a porter. Now that it could understand my words, I was able to give the golem instructions to perform simple tasks.

Winter came early that year, and the people in my town were suffering. Their weak, bony hands would freeze as they chopped and hauled wood for their stoves. But without wood to burn, the cold air in their homes would dig into their skin and choke their chests.

I reflected: I have fashioned a golem who has strong arms and does not feel the cold. Why shouldn't he chop and deliver wood to every household? No need for anyone in the town to suffer.

And so, I showed the golem how to gather and chop wood and then load it into the stove and light a fire. Once he had successfully repeated these tasks and lit my stove, I explained to him that his job was now to do the same for each household in our *shtetl*. At first, he was confused, as he did not understand what it meant to have a particular duty to perform. But I was able to teach him that gathering wood and lighting stoves was what he was supposed to do and that this had been his purpose in being created.

Finally understanding, the golem got to work. He chopped wood day and night, delivered it to every household, and lit a fire in each stove. The Jews in our town rejoiced—we were saved from the brutal winter. Everyone could remain snug and warm inside, and wait for the frost to thaw.

It took six days for the golem to chop and deliver wood to every household. When he was finished, I praised him for performing such a tremendous *mitzvah*. *Shabbat* was about to begin, and I told the golem that it was time to rest and pray.

But the golem now became upset. He said to me: My duty is to chop and deliver wood—is this no longer my task?

It was still his task, I assured him, but he could rest for a little while as everyone had enough wood for the next few days. When they would need more wood again, then he could go back to gathering and chopping and so on and so forth.

The golem, though, did not understand. He just repeated that his task was to chop and deliver the wood.

I sighed in frustration and left to pray my Friday evening prayers in the synagogue. The golem remained where he was, standing in my courtyard and repeating over and over again that it was his task to chop and deliver the wood. I figured he was a bit slow in the head, but I was not worried. After all, what trouble would he get into standing in my courtyard repeating the same few stupid words?

I should have been more careful—I should have never created that creature in the first place. For as I was concluding my prayers that Friday night, I suddenly heard screams coming from the street outside—Fire! Help! Fill the buckets with water!

I put down my prayerbook and left the synagogue. Two blocks from the main square there was a pillar of smoke and flames shooting up into the sky. I rushed over to help.

And what did my eyes see when I reached the house on fire? My golem was standing there with a pile of wood in his hands trying to enter the burning house, but his path was blocked by a crowd pleading with him to leave.

I went up to the golem and told him that this house needed water, not wood, because the water would put out the fire. We needed to go to the well and get some water.

But he refused to budge. His task, he said, was to deliver the wood. He had been delivering the wood and lighting the stove but then the people in the house had forced him outside. He now wished to go back inside so he could finish delivering the wood and lighting the fire.

I yelled at him: You *meshuggeneh* lump of clay—wood will only make the fire worse! And it will spread to other houses!

Then I was interrupted by a young girl who said that my golem was the one who had started the fire that was burning down her home—he had barged into the kitchen and shoved a pile of wood into the already full stove, causing several embers to fall out and spread their flames all over the kitchen floor.

I implored the golem to stop doing what he was doing—to try to understand that wood was good sometimes, but not always. So, sometimes it was his task to deliver wood but sometimes it would be better to deliver water.

But my words only enraged him more. He screamed even more loudly that it was his task to deliver wood. He must perform his task.

It was then that I understood that creating the golem had been a terrible mistake. The Holy One, Blessed be He, alone can create a full and complete human soul, with all three of its parts, including the *Neshama*, the intellect that gives men an understanding superior to beasts and birds. I had tried to draw down such a complete soul from the highest worlds and loftiest emanations of the *Ein Sof*, but I had lacked the strength needed to carry a complete soul with a *Neshama*. Instead, I had drawn down only the *Nefesh*, the material, animal soul, the soul of a stupid brute without comprehension.

I grabbed his arms to prevent him from entering any more houses with his piles of wood. He groaned and threw me to the earth with such force that my forehead cut open and bled. Still, I had enough presence of mind to reach for his leg and pull him down onto the ground beside me.

We had a terrible struggle, like Jacob and the Angel. He overcame me more than once. But I was always able to grab hold of him again just in time. When I was not sure how much longer my strength would last, I had the idea of rubbing away the *aleph* carved on his forehead, the first letter in the Hebrew word *Emet*. Without the *aleph*, the remaining letters would spell *Met*, which means death.

As soon as my finger smudged away the *aleph* on his forehead, the golem collapsed lifeless onto the ground. I grabbed a piece of firewood from his dead hands and used it to smash the golem's clay body into tiny bits. When I was finished, I scattered the fragments in a stream. And ever since that day, I have neither fashioned a golem nor taught any of my disciples how to do so.

So, hearing my tale, does Your Honor still wish for me to bring this doll back to life? Perhaps it would be better to enjoy the doll as something lovely to gaze upon now and then, but for a wife, maybe pick a flesh and blood woman?

Pan Jozef had sat quietly through Rabbi Eliyahu Baal Shem's tale. Now he spoke again, in a firm and commanding tone: Rabbi, thank you for recounting your memories. But that was *your* golem, with, as you concede, its own unique, deficient, stunted soul. I know the soul of my beloved. While some wicked rabbi, for reasons I cannot fathom, has chosen to rob her of the faculty of speech—at least for the time being—she still expresses the most refined sentiments through subtle shifts in her eyes. I have closely observed her pupils—how they expand and contract, when they tremble and when they are still, and how they ever so slightly move about from side to side. Our souls have become entwined through these subtle, but still potent, means. We have pledged our love to one another more deeply than through mere words—words that can carry deceptions and snares.

I know her soul. It is innocent and pure, virtuous and kind, loving and beloved. There is no danger. There is only the opportunity to free from silence and captivity one who knows nothing of guile or low cunning—a true child of nature, uncorrupted by an evil society that instructs its young women in the arts of avarice and treachery.

Accordingly, you are hereby instructed, Rabbi Eliyahu, to do what is necessary to bring my beloved back to a full human life. My Jewish subjects will be amply rewarded for your success. But if you fail, or if you refuse . . . Well, you understand.

V. Raising the Golem

ALTHOUGH ELIYAHU BAAL Shem realized he had no choice but to reanimate the doll, he at least took comfort in the fact that this golem was not going to be let loose among ordinary Jews, but instead, would be sharing this crazy nobleman's bed. Maybe the Holy One, Blessed be He, had decided to use this golem to punish *Pan* Jozef for his many sins. Who could say?

So, he told the nobleman that he would perform the ritual to bring the golem back to life. However, the process would take several days, as he must purify himself first. *Pan* Jozef readily agreed—whatever needed to be done would be done—no vital step skipped over.

For the next week, except during the holy *Shabbat*, Eliyahu fasted and prayed for forgiveness of his sins. He immersed himself twice a day in the waters of the *mikveh*. When the Jews of V. learned what Eliyahu Baal Shem had agreed to do for their sake, they too fasted for a day and recited Psalms in his honor.

Once he was purified of his sins, Eliyahu returned to *Pan* Jozef's manor house. He brought Rabbi Yitzhak along with him as well as two young men, stout blacksmith's apprentices, should he need help restraining the golem. They were all dressed in shimmering white *kittels* and they *davened* fervently in the back of the wagon that brought them to the nobleman.

Pan Jozef greeted them eagerly, and appeared to tremble with hope and excitement. Eliyahu ordered that the doll be removed from her case, taken to the cellar, and laid out across the floor atop a white sheet. Candles were to be lit all around her. He and the other Jews would pray by themselves while the nobleman's servants carried out these tasks.

After the sun had fallen and three stars were visible in the sky, Eliyahu called out to the steward to lead him and his companions down into the cellar. There, they found the doll lying upon the ground surrounded by an oval of softly burning candles. Eliyahu was struck again by how unnervingly lifelike the doll was—he could almost mistake her for a living woman.

Before Eliyahu could begin, the nobleman bounded down the cellar stairs and insisted that he be permitted to observe the proceedings, with his steward by his side. Eliyahu shrugged, and told him to remain in a far corner and not interfere, even if—or especially if—it appeared that Eliyahu's soul had departed from his body.

Eliyahu instructed the two blacksmith's apprentices to stand on either side of the doll's torso. Should she come to life and become a danger, they were to grab her arms and pin her to the ground. Rabbi Yitzhak was ordered to walk behind Eliyahu and repeat whatever words he uttered, no matter how bizarre, while concentrating intently on the image of the Hebrew letters as he was speaking them aloud.

Eliyahu took out his copy of the manuscript of Eleazar of Worms and flipped forward several pages. Then he started to slowly walk around the doll reciting different combinations of the names of the Holy One, Blessed be He, and His host of angels. After a couple of hours had gone by, he felt his limbs slacken. He forced his chanting and his steps to quicken; he invoked ever more powerful sacred names.

And then he felt his soul struggle to free itself from his body. The clawing and scratching of his soul against the prison of his old, wrinkled flesh knocked Eliyahu to the ground, and he felt blood trickle across his lips. His vision blurred and his mouth foamed.

A hand—an angel's hand—an angel whom he had summoned by name and bound to his will—reached into his flesh and pulled out his soul. Angel and soul soared together into the sky, past the stars and the constellations, and into Paradise, where the angel dropped Eliyahu's soul at the door to the Celestial Academy. But Eliyahu had not ascended so that he could hear words of Torah from the sages passing their eternity in the World to Come. No, he had to reach higher—he was still in far too lowly a place to draw down the divine flux needed to breathe a soul into a doll of clay and dirt.

He concentrated again on the most powerful and awesome true names for *HaShem*. Wielding the power of these names, he was able to vault himself higher, past Paradise, past the Heavenly Court and the Messiah's Palace and *Gan Eden*, until he beheld an immense throne, a structure so vast that it could contain thousands of worlds, millions of worlds. Upon this throne sat a giant, and from him sparks of light—sparks of pure creation—emanated in every direction, dazzling the dark sky with a wild illumination.

Eliyahu's soul groped for these sparks and tried to inhale as many of them as it could. But his soul was soon close to bursting, for such divine power could not be contained in such a flimsy, fragile vessel as a human spirit. Terrified that he would be consumed if he should linger any longer before the Throne of Glory, Eliyahu blocked all holy names from his mind and concentrated instead upon the things of the lowly material world—toads and ants, goats and chickens, mud splattering on a pair of boots, a drunken peasant puking in the harsh morning sun. And as he concentrated his thoughts upon these petty, base matters, his soul fell—slowly at first, but then faster, and faster still, until he was hurling downward at such a wild speed that he now feared crashing into the Earth.

Before he knew it, his soul collided violently with his body. He then sat up and rubbed his eyes. He saw that he was back in the cellar of *Pan* Jozef's manor house. He turned his eyes to the doll lying on the floor before him, opened his mouth, and belched loudly. The holy light that he had swallowed—and which had nearly seared him from within—streamed forth and enveloped the doll like a mist.

Once the holy sparks had departed from his soul, Eliyahu Baal Shem felt a great weariness overcome him and he collapsed into a deep slumber. When he awoke again, he was lying in a warm bed and the sun was shining brightly through an open window. He called out for help, for he felt too weak to rise by himself and he needed food and drink, now that he no longer was compelled to fast.

A few minutes later, a large crowd burst into the room, including the steward, Rabbi Yitzhak, the blacksmith's apprentices, and several servants. But then they all stood aside as *Pan* Jozef entered with a tall and graceful woman in a white gown.

The nobleman greeted him enthusiastically: My dear Rabbi Eliyahu, you have triumphed—you are indeed a master of the esoteric lore of your Israelite tradition. Let me introduce you to my fiancée, whom I have named Ewa. Look closely at her—you should recognize her.

Eliyahu slowly and gingerly sat up, as his old bones were horribly stiff and could no longer easily bear the bruising that came with his soul jumping in and out of his body. He squinted his eyes and looked closely at this Ewa. And then he did indeed recognize her: For Ewa was the doll from the glass case. She was a golem and he had brought her back to life.

Recalling his last golem—whom he could barely handle when he had been a young man full of vigor—Eliyahu felt a sudden terror. His fear, he realized, must have been written on his face, because the nobleman said: Why are you so pale and sullen, my good Rabbi?

Before you are the purest sentiments of love and affection, of sincere and unfeigned devotion. But perhaps you are merely hungry after all that fasting you were compelled to undertake? I am afraid, though, that my kitchen does not comport with the strict dietary laws of the prophet Moses. I will have you taken back to town shortly, where you may eat as much proper Jewish fare as you desire.

Nevertheless, I must insist that you remain on my lands for the time being, in case something should go awry with my beloved Ewa and your assistance be required once more. You shall stay as an honored guest at the house of Mendel, my Jewish leaseholder. I will make sure he receives ample funds to attend to all of your needs.

And with that, the nobleman left the room, with his adored golem still hanging on his arm. However, just as they were about to cross the threshold, Eliyahu saw Ewa turn her head around and look at him with eyes full of sadness and pleading—although for what she yearned, he did not know.

VI. A Brief Shtetl Idyll

AS IT TURNED out, Eliyahu enjoyed lingering in the *shtetl* of V. Reb Mendel, the wealthy leaseholder of *Pan* Jozef, proved to be a generous and kind host. He gave Eliyahu the use of a spacious bedroom, with a mattress so soft that Eliyahu felt it was a foretaste of the delights of Paradise. And then there was the food: Eliyahu quickly filled out his emaciated frame with succulent brisket and kugel and goose meat and borscht with thick sour cream and honey cakes and raisin cakes and who could even remember what other delicacies that streamed out of Reb Mendel's busy kitchen.

The company, too, proved welcome. Mendel had been a *yeshiva bochur* before his marriage to a wealthy merchant's daughter and still tried to study a page of *Gemara* each morning. Eliyahu Baal Shem now joined him as his daily study partner.

And that was not the only time when Eliyahu would study the holy texts. He would also study with Rabbi Yitzhak in the *bet midrash* later in the morning and counsel the judges of the local rabbinic court when they were faced with a particularly tangled problem of *halachah*. Soon enough, several Jewish householders begged him to teach their sons. While he refused all offers of payment—for, as he said, the merit of teaching the Torah was more than enough reward—Eliyahu agreed to lead a group of older boys in learning the Talmud.

In the midst of so much feasting and studying, Eliyahu Baal Shem sometimes almost forgot about the crazy nobleman and his golem fiancée. Nevertheless, from time to time, as they ate dinner or shared some brandy, Reb Mendel would relay the gossip he had picked up from *Pan* Jozef's steward and other retainers.

The Lady Ewa—for that is how His Lordship took to referring to the golem—could do no wrong in her lover's eyes. He showered her with clothes and jewels, and they went on long walks together in his woods and apple orchard. He wrote to all the other lords and ladies of the district announcing his engagement to Ewa, whom he described as a child of nature and an aristocrat of the spirit. Mendel had no idea how the other nobles were taking this strange news, but he supposed that at least none of them yet suspected that their fellow lord had fallen in love with a giant clay doll.

Then there was the delicate matter of Ewa's faith. Although Rabbi Eliyahu did not consider a golem to be a Jew—after all, a golem was not born from the womb of a Jewish mother and, in the case of male golems, would never be circumcised—*Pan* Jozef apparently disagreed and considered Ewa to be a Jewess. And while he did not feel any compunction about marrying a clay doll with no noble blood (or blood of any kind, for that matter), he told his steward that he could not suffer the scandal of marrying outside the Church. Thus, he declared, Ewa must be baptized a Catholic.

So, the nobleman told his priest to teach Ewa what she needed to know to become a Christian and then to baptize her. Once she was baptized, the wedding would follow shortly thereafter. But something went wrong. While Reb Mendel was not entirely sure of all the details, the priest apparently had refused to meet with Ewa again after two futile attempts to instruct her in his faith. He complained bitterly about her stiff-necked Jewish soul and urged His

Lordship to break off the engagement and find a proper Catholic lady to wed.

Pan Jozef ignored this counsel and instead wrote to the Bishop asking for a new priest. This new priest was a clever fellow. He said that the Lady Ewa would probably find it more agreeable to be tutored in Christian teachings by a fellow woman, and thus he cunningly evaded the snare that had felled his predecessor.

Pan Jozef dispatched Ewa to a convent that his ancestors had endowed, with instructions to the Mother Superior to educate Ewa about their Jesus and Trinity and all the rest. There were rumors, though, that this did not go well either, as the peasants who tended the convent's livestock swore they heard screaming and fighting and the sounds of plates being smashed coming from inside the nunnery walls.

But the nobleman insisted that he had received a letter—although he showed it to no one—from the esteemed and venerable Abbess assuring him that the Lady Ewa had been an eager and talented pupil of the Christian faith and quickly mastered all their teachings. Based upon the Mother Superior's alleged assurances, the new priest solemnly baptized Ewa in the local parish church, although she screamed when the Church holy water touched her clay golem's head.

Pan Jozef now resolved to move forward with the wedding. As a first step, he threw a grand ball to introduce Ewa to all the other lords and ladies in the district and whichever of his relatives might be inclined to make the trip. The preparations for the ball drove Reb Mendel to distraction, for he had to supply—and at below market prices!—enough vodka for all the guests and their coachmen and valets.

Reb Mendel was relieved when the night of the ball finally came around. After delivering the last barrels of vodka, he returned home and relaxed in his kitchen with a flask of mead that he shared with Rabbi Eliyahu. The two men shared memories of their children, when they were little and before they married and moved away, and the silly, funny things they used to say. Eliyahu recalled how one of his sons, then no more than three or four years old, had got it into his head that a goat they kept was being naughty and needed to be instructed in proper behavior—an unfortunately fruitless endeavor.

The next day, in the early afternoon, Mendel returned to the manor house to salvage whatever was left of his barrels of liquor. He did not return home again until late at night, long after everyone else had fallen asleep. At breakfast the following morning, Mendel recounted to Eliyahu the story of the ball as he had heard it from the steward who had been there:

Everything began well enough. The carriages pulled up to the veranda in front of the manor house, and the nobles poured out in all their finery. *Pan* Jozef mingled amongst his guests and cheered their spirits with glasses of vodka. The musicians played their music, a singer sang melancholy love songs in Polish, and a few old couples danced slowly and merrily.

And then came the moment that His Lordship had so eagerly anticipated: When he would slip away from his guests only to return triumphantly with his fiancée, the golem Ewa, hanging on his arm. She had been dressed that day by the finest tailors from Warsaw—upon whom *Pan* Jozef had showered a fortune to make his Ewa look as lovely as a princess—and her handmaidens had painstakingly styled and pinned her hair and painted her face with rouge and all the other cosmetic concoctions used by wealthy noblewomen to beautify their appearances.

When *Pan* Jozef re-entered the ball with Ewa by his side, his guests gasped melodramatically and heaped praises on her grace and loveliness. Then the nobleman ordered the musicians to strike up a light and playful tune, something he had heard before in Italy or France, and he began to dance with Ewa.

This did not go so well: No one had apparently thought about the fact that, as a golem and not a maiden reared in aristocratic manners, she had never been taught how to dance. She was clumsy, confused, stepped on her partner's feet, and nearly sent him crashing to the floor.

Muffled snickering sprang up all over the room. *Pan* Jozef grew visibly flustered, and gripped his beloved golem lady ever more tightly; the steward assumed this was to help her keep time to the music and follow his lead in the dance steps. But she must have misunderstood: For when he held her closely, she screamed in terror, knocked him to the ground, and ran away to a far corner of the room. She was not crying—as a golem, she did not have any tears in her eyes—but she moaned loudly and shamelessly, like a diseased cow.

A kindly old noblewoman went over to console her. Yet before that distinguished Lady could speak any words of comfort, Ewa jumped to her feet and slapped the old woman so hard that she fell hurtling to the ground and started bleeding all over her face. The grand ball then collapsed into chaos: Everyone ran for the doors, calling out for their drivers and coaches, and fleeing from what they called that madwoman Ewa. *Pan* Jozef, for his part, simply stood there dumbfounded. The steward eventually whisked him away to a safely isolated back bedroom, and directed a couple of the female servants to watch the Lady Ewa, from a discreet distance.

The next day, *Pan* Jozef said he was to blame for the Lady Ewa's violent outburst. She was an innocent child of nature, full of simple love and naïve virtue, and unaccustomed to the hypocrisies of polite society. When paraded before a crowd of treacherous and venal schemers, who flaunted their feigned sympathy, but were secretly brimming with the poisons of contempt and greed, the Lady Ewa had instinctively recoiled and sought her escape.

And so, later that same day, the nobleman apologized to his fiancée and swore once more his eternal and undying love. He promised never again to exhibit her before a mob of leering coquettes and libertines. Instead, they would wed in a modest, private ceremony in the family chapel in the manor house.

VII. The Wedding Night

ELIYAHU BAAL SHEM had not fully appreciated just how well he had been sleeping in Reb Mendel's luxurious bed until he was rudely awoken in the middle of the night. There were three men standing over him—Mendel, the nobleman's steward, and someone else, whom Eliyahu guessed was some other servant of His Lordship. They were all talking wildly with their hands flying about in frenzied gestures, and it took a few moments before their words cohered into any kind of sense.

Then he heard Mendel say: Rabbi Eliyahu, you must get out of bed at once. Your help is needed urgently—she has gone crazy—beating people, breaking furniture.

Eliyahu asked what had happened—why had the golem suddenly exploded into such a rage?

Mendel replied: Today was their wedding day, *Pan* Jozef and his Ewa. Everything was fine during the ceremony and the meal afterwards. But when the *Pan* brought her back to his bedroom, she ran screaming away from him. The servants found their lord naked, bleeding, and unconscious. You must go to the manor house with us right away and stop her from doing anything worse.

Eliyahu sighed and nodded. He had warned that fool nobleman. Did the stupid *Pan* really think a golem could make a decent wife, a helpmeet, for him? Still, the golem needed to be brought under control or, even better, broken into bits and the bits cast into a lake.

Eliyahu quickly washed, dressed, and squeezed into the back of the coach with Mendel and the steward (the third man being the driver of the carriage). Then they were off into the black night, with only a sliver of moon and a lantern on the coachman's box to guide their way.

When they arrived at the manor house, there was turmoil everywhere they looked — shouts and screams, servants heaving buckets of water on fires that had broken out in multiple rooms, doors knocked off their hinges, and piles of broken chairs and tables.

Where is she? Eliyahu asked.

The steward approached the broken doorway and called into the house, loudly repeating Eliyahu's question and then disappearing inside for several minutes. When he emerged again onto the veranda, he motioned for Eliyahu and Mendel to follow him.

They made their way through the debris and past a dying fire, down the main hallway, and finally to the room where *Pan* Jozef kept his collection of artifacts, specimens, and curiosities. There they came upon Ewa in an elegant white gown splattered with blood and torn on the side of one leg.

Fortunately, and unlike in his younger days, Eliyahu did not need to physically struggle with the golem. In the many years that had passed since the time when he had fashioned and destroyed his own golem, he had learned new great and awesome esoteric secrets, including how to command the higher spiritual powers to do his bidding in times of crisis. Rabbi Eliyahu thus now closed his eyes and concentrated on permutations of the holy name of a gruesome, avenging angel. The angel promptly answered his summons and, at Eliyahu's command, grabbed Ewa's arms from behind her back and lifted her up from the ground.

Speaking in Hebrew, Eliyahu directed the angel to brush the golem's hair away from her brow. He hoped to put Ewa to sleep as he had his own golem by erasing the Hebrew letters that had been inscribed on her forehead.

Ewa now spoke—the first time Eliyahu had heard her voice, which was softer than he had thought it would be. She said, also in Hebrew: Great Rabbi, Master and Teacher, please do not hurt me. I know what you intend to do—it has been done to me before. Please, I beg you, hear my plea: I have acted only to protect my modesty and honor as a Jewish maiden, as a daughter of Israel. That man wished to shame me and violate me. I am no danger to you or to any other righteous, upstanding man. Please, protect me from him.

Eliyahu replied: Did you not accept baptism, and agree to become his bride? It is permitted for a husband to lay with his wife upon their wedding night.

But I never agreed to be baptized, Ewa said. I am a Jew and he sought to defile me. Please, let me tell you my tale. Then you will understand; then everything will be clear to you. You are wise—so very wise—you remind me of my beloved father, may his memory be for a blessing. I know your heart will tremble with pity once you hear the truth from my lips.

Eliyahu was not sure what to do. What great tale of woe could a clay doll have? On the other hand, what harm was there in hearing her out? The angel was gripping her tightly, so she was not a danger anymore. And maybe he could discover something new about golems. It would be good to learn who had created her. He had never heard of a woman golem before, much less one so lifelike and pleasing to the eyes. Why create such a thing? To satisfy some base lust? But then why imbue her with a sense of honor and shame, as if she actually were a true-born daughter of Israel?

Eliyahu turned to his human companions. Switching from Hebrew to Yiddish, he asked them to leave him alone for a little while with the golem Ewa. When they protested that he was an old man and would be in grave danger should she become angry again, he answered that he was not afraid as he had availed himself of the powers of an angel bound to him through a secret and terrible holy name.

And so, Mendel, the steward, and a couple of other straggling servants left the room and closed the door behind them.

Eliyahu turned back to the golem and said to her, once more in Hebrew: Whatever you wish to say to me, say it now.

VIII. The Golem's Tale

THE GOLEM EWA began her tale, speaking in Hebrew: Master and teacher, gaon of our age, pillar of the generation, great rabbi, thank you for bending your ear to my words. I was created hundreds of years ago by a powerful and learned scholar of the *kabbalah*, a man of deep wisdom and wide learning. He had studied with Rabbi Eleazar of Worms of blessed memory, who taught him many secrets of the esoteric Torah. This scholar eventually settled down in the lands to the east of Worms, where he served as the rabbi of a small community. He married a local woman, a humble and pious daughter of a merchant. She would cry tears of joy each morning when she heard the sounds of her husband studying the Talmud.

They had a daughter, Hannah. She was the apple of her father's eye. And she was wise—so wise—and eager to learn. Her father instructed her in the laws that regulate women's conduct, so that Hannah, when grown, could teach the other women in the community and guide them in the path of righteousness.

They would speak together for hours, often long into the night. When his soul was full of bitterness or torment, his Hannah would comfort him. And when he was joyful, she shared in his joy.

Over time, Hannah blossomed into a beautiful maiden. The time came for her to be betrothed, and to become a wife and mother in her own right. There were many matches proposed for her, even without much of a dowry, for there were few Jewish maidens in that generation as lovely, modest, and pious.

And yet, her father could not bear the thought of being replaced by a husband. He knew this was wrong, and that his Hannah merited the blessings of marriage and motherhood. She looked at him with such hopeful eyes when the matchmakers visited their home. He knew his hesitation was wounding her, and bringing her sorrow. And yet . . . his heart broke at the thought of her leaving him.

Alas, he was fated to lose his Hannah no matter what. Armed men, on their way to *Eretz Yisrael* to join the other Christian knights who had taken Jerusalem, attacked his town. They burned the synagogue and slaughtered many Jews who died for *Kiddush Ha-Shem*, the sanctification of His Holy Name. Among the houses that the wicked men entered was his, my maker's. When they beheld Hannah's innocent, pure beauty, their lusts overcame them and they forced her down against a table and dishonored and shamed her. Her mother tried to stop them, but one of the wicked men drove his sword into her heart and made of her a martyr to Israel's long suffering in Exile.

Hannah begged them to stop, warning that this horrible sin would stain their souls and doom them to misery and torture in the next world. Her words must have angered them; once they had finished their shameful acts, their leader ran his sword through Hannah's belly. Then the wicked knights left the house, and went on their way.

And during all these horrible crimes, where was my father and maker, the powerful and learned kabbalist? He had hidden behind two barrels in a corner. He witnessed everything that was done to his wife and daughter, but fear seized his heart and he had been unable to muster the strength to try to help them. Afterwards, he was consumed by shame. His wife, a frail woman, had dared to raise her hand against the filthy Hamans, the evil beasts, who had shamed, and murdered his Hannah. But he had been too much of a coward.

He saw himself now as a great sinner—an arrogant fool puffed up with pride—and he was certain that his many sins had caused the sufferings of his wife and daughter. So, he gave up his rabbinate and all honor in this world. He fled to a hut deep inside the forest, where he lived on nuts and berries and water from a stream. He prayed day and night, begging the Holy One, Blessed be He, to forgive him and show mercy to the souls of his wife and his Hannah.

To help focus his mind upon higher, spiritual matters, he had brought several Hebrew manuscripts with him to the forest. These he stored in a dry barrel with a tight lid to keep them safe from the wind and the rain. Among the manuscripts were the teachings of his master Eleazar of Worms that revealed secret truths concealed beneath the surface meanings of the Torah. And among those secrets was the secret of making a golem from dirt and clay and breathing a soul into it.

He often pondered that teaching about golems. He was lonely in his hut, and often wept for hours at a time. But he did not long for the company of the Jewish householders whom he had left behind. No, he yearned for the daughter whom he had loved so deeply, for his Hannah. He missed how she would speak to him late into the night, even when he was so exhausted that he could barely keep his eyelids open. She would speak loudly and passionately of anything and everything—gossip, weather, animals, cooking, the *chazan*'s favorite melodies to chant in the synagogue, or her thoughts about the lessons to be learned from the examples of Sarah and Abraham, Rebecca and Isaac, and Rachel and Jacob. Hannah's noisy, incessant chatter—always accompanied by wild and dramatic movements of her hands—would weary him, and sometimes irritate him. Yet now it was the memory of those endless conversations that filled his soul with bitter longing and regret.

So unbearable was his loneliness that he resolved to use the teachings of Rabbi Eleazar to fashion a special balm for his suffering. He gathered dirt and clay and brought them into his hut. There, over the course of several days, he formed these materials into a lifelike statue of his Hannah. When it was finished and dried, he followed the rituals and invoked the holy names that Eleazar of Worms had prescribed and drew down a soul from the supernal realms which he breathed into the statue, bringing it to life as a golem.

I was that golem. I have trouble remembering my first days. I only see faint images—of my father, of the hut, of the trees. I recall being scared and trembling, but I had no words. And then he comforted me, and he held me, and I felt my fear fade away.

Soon enough, though, I learned to speak. My father taught me Hebrew first and then other languages. I have always been able to learn new languages. But Hebrew is the language of my heart. Once I was able to speak, my father taught me all about the world and the Torah.

He also taught me all about his Hannah, their life together, how she had been shamed and murdered, and how he had come to the forest hut to repent of his many sins. I felt a terrible sadness when I learned all that he had suffered, and I swore to ease the burden of his loneliness and sorrow.

I loved him and cared for him. I gathered and prepared his food, and I brought him water from the stream. At night, when the moonlight streamed into our hut, I spoke to him in just the way— or at least so I hoped—that his Hannah had once spoken to him. I spoke about anything I could think of, and I saw that my chatter and my flapping hands warmed his heart and brought him joy.

One day I asked him if he was going to die and if I was going to die. I did not understand death well, but I had heard him speak of people dying, like Hannah, and I had seen beasts and birds die many times. He told me that his soul would soon leave his body and ascend to the World to Come to be reunited with his wife and daughter.

But as for me, I was a golem. The Angel of Death would not come for me because I had not been created by the Holy One, Blessed be He. I would continue to wander this lowly world forevermore.

I cried out in agony at these words. If I had tears in my clay body, they would have gushed forth like a mighty river. I asked how he could create me, and show me the tenderest love of a father for his daughter, only to leave me alone and wretched for all eternity.

In response, he hung his head and sighed. He was quiet for a long time. When he spoke again, he said I was right—it had been an act of cruelty to endow me with a soul only to abandon me to an eternity of longing for a father with whom I could never be reunited. To ease my future sufferings, he decided to fashion a companion for me. He directed me to gather and bring him a huge quantity of dirt and clay from the banks of the nearby stream. After I had done so, he and I worked together to fashion a new clay statue, this time of him. When we had finished, he took out the manuscript of Eleazar of Worms and once more performed the ritual and recited the holy names that brought down a soul into the clay body. And thus, a second golem was born—a golem of him, a golem to be a father to me and to love me and whom I could care for and love in return, forevermore.

Shortly before the Angel of Death came for him, my creator copied out Eleazar of Worms' manuscript onto small pieces of parchment that I had procured from a nearby town, and placed them around our necks. He told us that, should something ever go wrong, we were to show these amulets to the most learned Jew whom we could find. A true scholar of the Torah would always aid us in our time of need.

Our creator fell asleep one night and was dead by morning. But his face was smiling with such hope—perhaps he had seen his Hannah again. We two, my golem father and I, buried him near the hut and, in our unlearned way, we said what prayers we could for the rest and safekeeping of his soul.

That night we both felt a terrible, aching despair. We had never been without our maker before. He had been kind, and always had something new to teach us. Yet now we were cursed to carry on, forevermore, without him. Still, we found comfort in each other.

We lived on together in the forest. It was an easy, simple life, for as golems we did not need food or drink. We occupied our time in building our house. At first, we merely fixed what was broken in the hut. Then we decided to enlarge it, so that the hut would become a proper house, even a fine and luxurious house. We cut down trees, chopped the wood, and built floors, walls, roofs, room after room. We also built furniture—beds, chairs, tables, and couches.

We would pick fruit or kill wild boars and sell them in the nearby towns. With the money we earned, we bought the things we could not make ourselves, such as candles, tablecloths, mattresses, and bed linens. Soon enough, we had constructed a mansion that would be the envy of any nobleman.

But our peace and solitude were not to last. Men began to find us—or sometimes we found them. It was often during a storm, and some youth had become lost. His horse was lame or dead, and he was shivering with hunger, thirst, and disease. He would knock on our door late at night, seeking shelter from the rain and the wind. Or sometimes we would find him the next morning after the tempest, his body and soul barely still together, lying wretchedly next to a tree stump.

We would take these men in, feed them, warm them, and nurse them back to health. We enjoyed their company. They would tell us of their lives and towns back home. Some were from famous cities.

We gave them life and health, and they gave us happiness and taught us many new things.

But then a change would come over them. As their sickness faded and strength returned, they would begin to look at me in a different way. Sometimes this look was tender and full of yearning. Other times it was a pulsating, salivating hunger.

These looks would be followed by declarations of love. They would ask for my hand in marriage, and praise my beauty and my kind heart.

Their praises filled me with dread. I felt no love for these men. I loved only my father—the golem of my creator—who was my companion in the forest. I loved him as no daughter has ever loved her father. The heart that my maker, of blessed memory, had fashioned for me could feel only a daughter's love for a father and no other. That daughterly love also compelled me to care for those in need of aid—for that was what Hannah would have done, and my task was to be a new Hannah. Yet unlike Hannah, I never wanted to be a bride—in this one detail alone, my creator had made me different—had made me a Hannah more as he had yearned for her to have been.

Sometimes the men would touch me, on the thigh, or hand, or cheek. Their touch burned me like a hot coal. I would flee to my golem father's arms, and he would embrace me and comfort me. He would ask what troubled me? And I would tell him—the confessions of love, the greedy touches.

He would then rebuke the men for abusing his hospitality by their filthy, shameful actions. His stern words would cool the blood of the decent, righteous men. They would apologize and ask for forgiveness, and speedily part from us, quietly and honorably.

Unfortunately, there were also other men, wicked men. They would insist that I had acted in subtle but unmistakable ways to arouse their lusts and lure them into their confessions of love. Sometimes they called me a lying whore. Other times they would swear that I had clearly returned their affections. They would often threaten harm to my golem father to force him to consent to giving me away in marriage.

I trembled in terror. My maker, my true flesh and blood father, had molded my golem father in his image: As a weak and frail old man, exactly as I had known him and loved him as his daughter. But because he had been fashioned to be weak, I knew that he would not survive a struggle with one of these young, vigorous men.

And so, to keep him safe, I would pretend to return their love but insist that my honor required that we not touch one another until after we were lawfully and properly wed. I would also say I could not marry unless I was sure my suitor's family had no objection to the match. I would ask that they leave me and send word to their families. Once I was confident of their family's blessing, then they could return and claim me as their bride.

This ruse worked well, for the forest protected us: We were far enough away from any road or town or even farm that once the young man had departed, he would never again be able to find his way back to us. And then I could continue to live in peace with my golem father.

Yet my happiness was eventually shattered. One night, during a horrible storm, a young man, barely alive, pounded on our door. As soon as we brought him inside, he collapsed onto the floor. His clothes were soaked through, he had a raging fever, and his teeth were chattering. Over the next several weeks, I nursed him back to health. He told me that he came from a large and famous city called Vienna. He told me fantastical tales of his Vienna—of a magical drink he called chocolate, and of music and theaters and a grand palace that housed a mighty empress and her sumptuous court. It all sounded so extraordinary that I was not sure whether this Vienna was even a real place.

Like the others, he declared his love for me and sought my hand in marriage. As with the others, I demurred and tried to trick him into leaving. But he would not depart without me. When I refused, he approached my golem father and asked him to accompany us to Vienna, as he was sure that my hesitations were out of fear for leaving my father alone in the woods. My father, however, recoiled in terror, swearing he was too old and frail for such a long journey.

Now the young man from Vienna grew suspicious. He accused my father of using my charms to toy with the hearts of wealthy men, intent, no doubt, on stealing their money. He said that while I played the innocent child of nature, I was in truth the most depraved and cunning coquette whom he had ever encountered—far more vicious than the cold, painted beauties who stalk the salons of Paris.

In response, my father defended my honor, and rebuked his young guest for not being properly grateful for all we had done for him. Instead of hurling insults, he should have been apologizing and politely taking his leave.

The young man seethed at these words and threw my father to the ground. I rushed over to help, but before I could, he had put his hand on my golem father's forehead and accidentally smudged the Hebrew letters that our maker had inscribed there. As soon as the letters were erased, my golem father fell limp, an empty vessel without a soul. Once his features had faded, it became clear he was merely a huge clay doll.

The young man cried out in terror and accused me of witchcraft. He said that I had enchanted him so that I could acquire his substantial fortune through marriage, after which, he was certain, I would poison his dinner and hand his riches over to my coven of she-devils and satanic whores.

Seeing my golem father on the ground, as if dead, shattered my heart. I could not bear the thought of being without him—particularly if I should wind up the prisoner of his murderer, this wretched, horrible young man. So, I reached out for my own forehead and felt for the slight indentations where my maker, my flesh and blood father, had carved the Hebrew letters into my clay skin. I rubbed against them until I felt my body go limp and numb, and then crash to the ground.

Just as my maker had warned me, the Angel of Death never came for my soul. Even though my clay body was lifeless, I, as a soul, remained trapped inside of it. I could not move or speak, and everything I saw was filtered through a film of shadow and fog. Sounds still reached me, but as distant, hollow echoes. I comforted myself with memories of my two fathers. I recalled their kindly smiles and how they would listen to me prattle on in the evenings, so patiently, so full of love.

And then one day, I returned to life with a sudden new strength in my limbs. My eyes saw clearly again, and my ears could discern every sound. You were standing over me, Rabbi Eliyahu. For a brief moment, I thought you were my golem father and that he had rescued me from oblivion. You resemble him so much—perhaps it is the white beard and *payes*. But as I looked harder—as my eyes adjusted again to seeing—I realized you were not him.

I looked around for my father, hoping he was somewhere nearby. Maybe you were his friend, sent to help me? I longed to be with him again, to love him and care for him in our house in the forest. But he was gone. I don't know what that man from Vienna did to him, or where he left him. I only hope that his soul, unlike mine, was able to make the journey to the World to Come.

And then you left me too. You abandoned me to another one of these horrible young men, this Polish nobleman Jozef. He forced me to be baptized. After I had been taught by my master and teacher, my flesh and blood father, the beauty and the truth of the Torah and the sweet teachings of the holy sages of blessed memory, the pain of being forced to bow down to the false gods and idols of this man's Church was unbearable.

Then he paraded me in front of his fellow nobles. I hated the way they looked upon me, and I pushed them away. My heart groaned in bitterness and sorrow, and I longed for my father—my Jewish father.

The worst, though, was that this Jozef married himself to me, in a ceremony performed by one of his priests. And then he took me to his bed. He stripped off my clothes, and pressed his flesh against mine. I felt sickened—I am not sure the right words to use—it was the most awful feeling I have ever felt—as if slimy maggots were squirming all over my skin.

I screamed and begged for him to stop. But he kept repeating that I was his wife now, and that if I merely relaxed my muscles and allowed my nerves to calm, I would soon be feeling the most exquisite pleasure.

But there was no pleasure. The hideous, terrible feeling only grew worse.

I begged again for him to stop. He rebuked me for my coldness and ingratitude after he had brought me back to life and raised me to a high rank with an enviable fortune. How could I repay his love and devotion, which he had proved repeatedly, with such cruelty—and on our wedding night!

I had to escape from him.

And so, Rabbi Eliyahu, having heard my tale, please do not force me back into the bed of this evil, idol-worshipping man. Let me live a life of simple piety and righteousness, with my heart overflowing with devotion to the Holy One, Blessed be He and His Torah.

Eliyahu Baal Shem thought: Although she was a golem, she was still a daughter of Israel, unyielding in her faithfulness to the Torah. She had spurned riches and titles—not just now but many times before—to remain true to *HaShem*. This soul—however it had come to be inside the clay doll's body—was a special, pious soul, a delicate and lovely flower. Her original father and maker must have been a scholar of great holiness to have been able to draw down such a rare and beautiful soul to be his golem daughter.

On the other hand, she had erased the Hebrew letters that had been inscribed on her forehead and had thus, in the manner of a golem, attempted to kill herself. Suicide is a terrible sin. As Moshe Rabbeinu taught in the Torah: I offer you a choice between life and death—choose life.

And so, Eliyahu said to the golem Ewa: You are a righteous and honorable daughter of Israel, willing to suffer for the Sanctification of His Holy Name. Still, your act of rubbing the letters off your forehead was a sin, for which you must atone. I will have the angel who holds you now return you to your former home in the forest. If it should be in disrepair, then the angel shall fix it for you. I urge you to spend your days in prayer and repentance.

Then Eliyahu Baal Shem closed his eyes and concentrated upon the secret true name of the angel and engaged in combinations of the letters of that name to compel the angel to do as he wished. When he opened his eyes again, both the angel and the golem were gone.

IX. To Love a Daughter of Israel

ELIYAHU BAAL SHEM did not remain much longer in the *shtetl* of V. He told *Pan* Jozef that the golem Ewa had overpowered him and run away—to where, he could not say. However, the nobleman, still recovering from his wounds, was not upset at her departure. He mused that Ewa had not been the pure child of nature for whom he had longed, and that her all too apparent shortcomings doubtless derived from being a creature forged by, and thus beholden to, backward Jewish superstitions from the Middle Ages. Nevertheless, as he now knew that it was indeed possible to create an artificial bride, he merely needed to figure out how to craft one more appropriate for a man of enlightenment and learning. He would consult again with his brothers in his secret society—surely one of them must have an inkling of the requisite esoteric knowledge. He pronounced himself finished with rabbis and Jews. Eliyahu was free to return to his faraway home.

And so, Rabbi Eliyahu left *Pan* Jozef's manor house. Upon his return to the town, he relayed to the community elders of V. all that had happened and his hope that the nobleman would now leave his Jews alone to live their lives in peace. He hinted that he might consider remaining in V., as the householders there had been so hospitable. But Reb Mendel made clear that, as *Pan* Jozef was no longer compensating him for the cost of housing and feeding Eliyahu, he would need to find a new home, at his own expense. Nor was anyone else in the community interested in taking on the burden of an old man.

With a heavy, melancholy sigh, Eliyahu Baal Shem journeyed home to the *shtetl* of C. At first, the Jews in his town were riveted by his wild tale of the golem bride and the *meshuggeneh* Polish lord. But after the third or fourth telling, they lost interest and drifted away.

Once more, Rabbi Eliyahu found himself alone on his porch, rocking on a bench and half-studying a tractate of the *Gemara*. At the synagogue, he would exchange coldly polite greetings with the other men. Although he tried to converse with them, he could see their minds were elsewhere. The householders were caught up in their business intrigues—matters in which old men with their creaky bones and creaky minds did not take part.

In his loneliness, his thoughts drifted to the golem Ewa. She could have chosen a life of wealth and luxury as a nobleman's bride. An army of servants would have waited on her hand and foot. She would have worn the finest dresses, and ridden in the most elegant carriages. She would have traveled to the mightiest cities of Europe and danced with kings and princes in their palaces.

But her heart—her clay and dirt heart—was so full of love for the Holy One, Blessed be He, that she would not betray Him and His Torah for all the riches that the crazy *Pan* Jozef was ready to shower upon her head. In her way, she had martyred herself for *Kiddush HaShem*—for the sanctification of His Holy Name.

Eliyahu wondered how Ewa was faring. Had she returned to her simple life in the forest? Was she devoting herself to prayer and repentance?

So, one afternoon, when the pains of loneliness were particularly sharp, he resolved to visit her. He closed his eyes tightly and concentrated on the holy name of the angel who had taken her back to her old home in the woods. When the angel duly appeared, Eliyahu said he wished to travel to the golem Ewa.

The angel grimly nodded, and enveloped Eliyahu in his soft golden wings. Then they bolted high into the air, above the clouds, and dashed briefly across the cold but brightly lit horizon before landing in a forest near a stream.

Once he had his bearings, Eliyahu turned around and beheld an elegant house nestled within a grove of birch trees. At first, he hesitated—for how could he be sure this was the golem's house? Maybe it was a robbers' den—or worse? But then again, what would robbers want with him? To steal the grey hairs from his beard?

So, he strode up to the door and knocked loudly. He heard a slight rustling from inside the house, followed by footsteps. A moment later the door swung open.

And there she was, the golem Ewa. She blushed and stammered when she saw Rabbi Eliyahu. She asked how he had found her.

He answered: By summoning the same angel who brought you back here.

She laughed nervously, invited him inside, and offered him a chair.

The interior of the house was simple, but welcoming. The walls and floor were bare, but carefully sanded down and spotlessly clean. It was dark—the curtains were drawn and the sun was setting—but warm from the fire smoldering in the hearth.

The golem Ewa sat down across from him. She said: Rabbi, as you instructed me, I pray as best I can, and I have pleaded with *HaShem* to forgive me for the sin of attempting to take my own life. But I am not a scholar, and I worry that I do not know the right words in the holy tongue, in Hebrew, to address my petitions to the Throne of Glory. It is hard to be alone.

Those last words stirred Eliyahu's heart, and he burst into loud, wailing sobs. Although he was ashamed at the spectacle he was making of himself, he was like a little boy again who cannot stop himself from crying out for his mother's breast.

The golem stood up, walked over, and embraced Eliyahu tenderly. She rocked him in her arms and cooed to him. Her voice and her touch washed away his pain, and he let his head rest against her rough clay skin.

After a few minutes, she let him go and returned to her seat.

Eliyahu said: My apologies—I should not have acted in such a shameful way. I came here to offer you comfort, and perhaps to instruct you. And yet instead, you comforted me. I am sorry—I suppose I can be a foolish old man.

The golem Ewa assured him there was no cause to be ashamed. She, too, knew the pain of loneliness. Only her clay body had no tears inside it. She envied him his tears.

That evening, Eliyahu sat with the golem Ewa in her home. He spoke to her about how to pray, and taught her different prayers. By the time he was finished, he was nodding off in his chair. Ewa helped him to stand and walk to an empty bedroom. This bed, she explained, was once her flesh and blood father's bed; then it was her golem father's bed. He could sleep there tonight, beneath the thick woolen blankets.

Eliyahu Baal Shem did not resist and happily let himself be fussed over and tucked in. The golem Ewa sat with him, smiling warmly and chatting softly about the birds and the weather, until sleep overcame him.

When he awoke the next morning, the sun was already high in the sky. As he started to rustle himself out of bed, he heard Ewa enter. She was carrying a tray with pastries and tea.

Eliyahu marveled at her devotion. She was a good, pure, kind soul. She yearned to honor and cleave to the Holy One, Blessed be He, and to ease the pains of a lonely old man. She was as innocent and gentle as Rebecca at the well, may the memory of the righteous be for a blessing.

After breakfast, Eliyahu prayed his morning prayers as Ewa stood by and watched. He could feel the awe and admiration in her gaze, and this filled his heart with pride. He remembered when his sons were small, and how they too would watch him pray with that same look of awe and admiration.

When he was finished, he summoned the angel again. The angel promptly reappeared and asked if he was ready to return home. Although he had planned to leave, Eliyahu suddenly felt a heavy dread at the thought of returning to the loneliness of his abode in the *shtetl* of C.

He looked over at Ewa. Her eyes were downcast and sorrowful.

Eliyahu told the angel he was not returning home but was going to remain with Ewa. He commanded the angel to gather his books, clothes, *tfillin*, and *tallit*, and bring them to the house in the woods. Once he had completed those tasks, the angel would then be responsible for making sure the house was properly provisioned with food and drink.

The angel groaned and muttered bitterly about the never-ending demands of the *tzaddikim*, but he did as he was told.

Ewa rushed over to Rabbi Eliyahu, embraced him, and said: You are my new father and I am your new daughter. We will stay together, and we shall be happy.

And so they did. With the angel's grudging but reliable assistance, Eliyahu lived a life that he thought must be a foretaste of the delights of Paradise. He studied and prayed, and doted on the golem Ewa as if she were his own daughter. And she listened to him, and learned from him, and doted on him in turn as if he were her elderly father.

But after several weeks of this idyll, the sky suddenly darkened one afternoon and the air turned bitter cold. The grey clouds unleashed a torrent of rain, which the vicious wind hurled and struck against the trees and the house and any animal unlucky enough to be out walking. Booming thunder and wild streaks of lightning quickly followed.

Ewa closed the shutters and brewed hot tea to warm Rabbi Eliyahu's bones. They sat calmly and silently together in the parlor room, listening to the howls and groans of the terrible storm raging just outside their door.

Then came a loud knock—so loud that they heard it clearly through the wind and the rain and the thunder. Ewa jumped up from her chair and opened the door to find a shivering young man soaked through his elegant, expensive clothes. His teeth were chattering, and his eyes were bloodshot and vacant.

Ewa dragged him inside, pulled off his wet clothes, and wrapped his naked body in a dry, warm blanket. She gave him a cup of tea and sat him down by the fireplace. He thanked her profusely and asked if she was an angel of God, sent in answer to his prayers.

Within a few minutes, he had fallen into a deep sleep and was snoring merrily.

Eliyahu Baal Shem did not like this young man. He recalled what the golem Ewa had told him about how such wealthy young gentlemen would become lost in storms and come to her for help—and how they would later fall in love with her and threaten to spoil the happiness of both her and her father.

So, he suggested to Ewa that he summon the angel again, and order him to take this young man back to wherever his home might be. The young man would no doubt think the house in the forest had been a wild dream brought on by his fever. And Eliyahu and Ewa could continue to live as they had been living without worrying about whether the new visitor would try to take Ewa away, as so many others had tried before.

Ewa, however, replied: Your words are sinful. We must help him. How can we know if he will be safe at his home? Maybe he has fled from his home. Or maybe, if he is a nobleman—which he appears to be—he has many homes, and the angel returns him to the wrong bed in the wrong one? No, let us heal him together and when he is strong again, then he may depart and choose his destination.

But Eliyahu protested: How can you not remember how so many young men whom you took in and healed then desired you as a wife and tried to take you away?

Ewa, though, would not budge. She was sure this young man would be different. And how could she abandon someone who was suffering so wretchedly? She had been made, by her maker, the great kabbalist master, to ease the pain of men just as that master's own daughter had eased his pains. And that is what she would do.

Eliyahu sighed and went to bed. What could he do with a stubborn golem? At least for now, the young man was harmless enough—he could barely stand up in his misery. And maybe Ewa was right and he would be different? Who could say?

For the next few weeks, Ewa nursed the young man back to health. As he was bedridden, he did not disturb Eliyahu's prayers or studies, and sometimes Eliyahu even forgot he was there. But little by little the young man recovered his strength until one day Eliyahu saw through the window of his bedroom that the young man was accompanying Ewa on a stroll by the nearby stream. He was walking slowly and gingerly; she helped him by holding his arm. He was blushing and smiling, and his gaze never moved from Ewa's lips and eyes. Eliyahu Baal Shem trembled with dread as he watched them.

When they returned home, Ewa guided the young man back to his bed to rest some more. After she gently closed the door to his room, Eliyahu told her that he wished to speak with her, and led her to the parlor room by the fireplace.

He said: I saw the way that young man was looking upon you. It is time that he should depart. No good will come of this—only evil.

But Ewa protested: The young man was not yet fully recovered; he needed more time. How could they just let him wander back off into the forest when he was still so sick?

Eliyahu replied: He will not wander. I will summon the angel who will carry him home. The young man will awake in his own bed, with his own family to comfort him and nurse him.

No—Ewa screamed—you cannot do that—how do we know they will care for him—they could be base, wicked people—they could harm him—

But Eliyahu was no longer paying attention to Ewa. He took a deep breath and closed his eyes. He concentrated in his mind on the secret holy name of the angel. Then his lips began to utter the combinations of the angel's true name that summon and bind him. But before Eliyahu could finish speaking the necessary words, he felt something push him to the ground. His head and back crashed to the floor with a hard thud and a terrible pain shot down his neck.

Opening his eyes, Eliyahu Baal Shem saw the golem Ewa on top of him, a furious terror in her eyes. He opened his mouth to start to speak, but she covered his lips with both her hands. Her grip was tight, and desperate. As she adjusted her fingers frantically, one of her palms fell hard on Eliyahu's nostrils.

He could not breathe. He tried to wriggle away, but she had pinned him down too well—his old, arthritic limbs were no match for her strength. Soon enough, though, he stopped feeling the pain of being suffocated.

And then he beheld a tall, black-cloaked figure arise above him—the Angel of Death with his hundred eyes had come to reap his soul.

Other Books by Barak Bassman

About the Author

Barak A. Bassman received a B.A. in Classics from Grinnell College and a law degree from the New York University School of Law. He practices law in Philadelphia, Pennsylvania, and lives in the Philadelphia suburbs with his wife and two children.

He is the author of, among other works, *Repentance: A Tale of Demons in Old Jewish Poland*, *King Solomon and Ashmedai: A Wisdom Tale*, *Necromancy of the Demon Maiden: A Gothic Tale of Podolia*, *The Vampire and the Wandering Jew*, *The Emissary from Mezeritch: A Dark Hasidic Tale*, *The Holy Sinner: A Gothic Tale of the Baal Shem Tov*, *The Baal Shem Tov and the Heretic: A Sabbatean Tale*, *The Starvation Dybbuk: A Cruel Tale of Love and Exorcism*, *The Twisted Path of the Hidden Saint: An Occult Tale of the Baal Shem Tov*, *The Mad Disciples of Jacob Frank: A Tale of the Demon Goddess*, and *The Descent of the Tzaddik: A Saint's Tale*.